KU-022-584

Contents

ACKNOWLEDGEMENTS

This book represents the sum of my experiences over half a century and would not have been possible without the input and help of many people.

The biggest influence were my parents, Jeanne and Martin, who not only provided the genetic input but also the perfect environment for three young boys to pursue a life in sport. It was a warm, loving environment full of care and support and well-considered advice at critical moments. I have no doubt that the nurture was more important than the nature in our case.

Having an older brother is a mixed blessing. The lessons, particularly the coping skills, I learned in those backyard tests matches stood me in great stead many years later when confronted by one of the greatest bowling attacks ever to have been played. There is no doubt in my mind that I would not have survived through that period without the apprenticeship I received in our backyard. Ian also provided the path for me to follow. He was my idol and his success in cricket provided me with the inspiration to develop my own talents. Without his example, I doubt that I would have believed it was possible for me to play cricket for Australia. Trevor, on the other hand, provided me with the opportunity to experience some success as I graduated to the older brother role. He also taught me some worthwhile lessons. Not least was how to run faster after I had pushed him too far and he came after me with a small axe.

I consider my coach Martin's input was invaluable. His common sense approach and insight into the nuances of the game set a great foundation. His friend Lynn Fuller also helped fuel the fire. I can't believe that I was so keen as a five-year-old to go to Lynn's on a Sunday morning to stand in line for my chance in the nets. His quiet manner and studied advice were a great help.

Chester Bennett and Prince Alfred College in Adelaide played an enormous part. Chester was a wonderful man and the perfect mentor for a boy who was eager to learn. Some of his lessons have proven to be my most valuable learning experiences. Ashley Woodcock, Jack Waters and Sandy Rhodes helped a shy boy from the western suburbs to settle into what was, for me, a daunting environment.

The Glenelg Cricket Club and stalwarts such as Des Selby, Brian 'Tom' Rundle and Sam Starling provided excellent support and a firm hand when required. My stint at Somerset County Cricket Club offered an opportunity to play under very different conditions at a critical stage of my development.

Teammates in South Australia, such as Ashley Mallett and Terry Jenner, were as fanatical as me and the hours we spent playing, training and living cricket also provided much needed encouragement. John Maclean and Tony Dell, teammates in Queensland, provided the opportunity and the belief that we could make a difference to cricket in the Sunshine State. John McKnoulty and the South Brisbane Cricket Club made it feel like home.

Dennis Lillee and Rod Marsh were the two with whom I started and ended my international career. I spent more time with them for fourteen years than I did my own family. Their honesty, advice and their efforts through those years are much appreciated. Jeff Thomson came along a few years later, and his honesty and humour made many a frustrating day much more bearable. He is the fastest, and most fearsome, bowler I have seen.

I consider myself fortunate to have played in an era when we had to have a career outside of sport. The lessons I learned on the cricket field have stood me in great stead off it, and vice versa.

People like Bruce Calman, Lyell Wilson, Barry Maranta, Bill Buckle and Ron McConnell have been great supporters and have given me the opportunity to achieve things off the field that I could not have done without their friendship and support. Barry and Lynn Maranta became the family that we did not have when we moved to Brisbane and started our own family.

Golf has become my passion after cricket and has helped channel my competitive energies. It has also taught me much about learning and understanding human movement because it must be one of the toughest sporting challenges there is, mentally as much as physically. People like Bob Barraket, Gerry Hogan and Tony Hutton have provided me with insights that have helped my golf and my understanding of how the brain and body work in unison.

Jack Clarke and Trevor Robertson from the South Australian Cricket Association can take much of the credit for this book for without their decision to tempt me back to Adelaide to a coaching role in cricket, I would not have become fascinated with how the development process in cricket has changed since I grew up. The frustration and pleasure that I got from working with a wonderful bunch of young men at the SACA provided the impetus that led to the research for this book. Tim Nielsen, who became my assistant coach in Adelaide, provided the youthful enthusiasm I needed to develop some of the ideas that appear on these pages. Without his energy and creative input many of these ideas would not have been given the oxygen they needed to grow.

The critical contact I made during this period though was to re-acquaint myself with Ian Frazer. I knew Ian when he played for Victoria but we had gone our separate ways. Through our mutual friend Swan Richards, we met up again and began sharing ideas on cricket coaching. Ian was coaching juniors in Melbourne and was encountering some of the same frustrations I was finding in my role in Adelaide. Swan suggested we get together because we had expressed similar ideas. Without Ian's vast library of books and videos it would not have been possible to do our research on what made the great players great.

The fact that Ian had played the game to a high level and had studied sports science made him the ideal foil to my 'bush lawyer' brand of science. The thing I gained most from the partnership with Ian was the confidence to back my intuition. He was able to explain to me why what I believed from my own experiences was correct. This helped me a great deal in my role with South Australia and has inspired me to understand more. This book is the culmination of my playing and coaching experiences and Ian's vast knowledge of sports science and human expression through sport.

Pam Brewster managed the process from the embryo of an idea, through the writing process, to the finished article. Her partner Rob Francis put our ideas into the cogent form that they appear on these pages. It has been a labour of love for Rob and I can't thank him enough for the hours that he has toiled to make sense of what I wanted to put into print.

None of this would have been possible without the support and love of my long-suffering wife and family. Judy has been with me through a marathon partnership that has spanned 33 years and has survived a few dropped chances and near run outs. Thankfully she has not given up on me and has provided me with the stability at home to allow me to pursue my passions. She also blessed me with three wonderful children and has given them the stability that a sporting lifestyle made difficult. I know Stephen, Belinda and Jonathan, like me, are grateful for her strength and wisdom. Judy's sister Elizabeth must take some of the credit, for it was she who introduced Judy and I in the first place while Judy's parents, Harry and Barbara, have been like the joint twelfth man and have carried the drinks lovingly through thick and thin and we all love them for it.

Foreword

Greg Chappell has always been a man who has had an inquisitive mind. It comes as no surprise that he would want to know what makes a good cricketer and it also comes as no surprise that he would study the best in the world to uncover the secrets of their success.

He has done just that in his book, *Greg Chappell on Coaching*. It is a very different cricket book and combines theories on the game which are closely aligned to everyday life. For example, the relatively simple act of walking can be aligned to batting, in more ways than one. I should explain that to a new walker, it isn't really a simple task, and to a new cricketer, I would imagine batting isn't all that easy. Fascinating stuff!

Greg was a highly successful player for a number of reasons. His technique was sound, his ability was well above average but most of all he had a very strong mental game. He was brought up in a very competitive environment and he learnt mental toughness at an early age. The mind has a great part to play in this wonderful game and those who master their own mind usually have a significant advantage.

In this book, you can actually get inside Greg's mind and find out just what he did to ensure success. You will find this fascinating and yet not difficult to understand.

Greg has covered all aspects of the game in this publication. He talks about technique, fitness and nutrition, captaincy and leadership, coaching, administration and the mind. He does this in a manner you will not find in other cricket books. It is an intriguing read and a book which will be widely read and discussed in the decades to come.

ROD MARSH

INTRODUCTION

The New Art of Cricket

An open heart and an open mind are all you need
to reach your full potential in life.

This book is about learning and perfecting the art of playing cricket. I wanted to write it because I believe it opens the doors to a number of secrets about playing and understanding the game — secrets that have been locked away since Don Bradman first alluded to them in his classic coaching book *The Art of Cricket*, published fifty years ago. I had the honour of knowing Bradman, the greatest batter of all time, and I believe he understood the fundamentals of what I discuss in this book. He certainly played as if he knew them.

In this book you will discover a very different approach to learning and perfecting the game. It is based on five theories that I call the *five critical pathways to success*.

1 **THE CORE PRINCIPLES OF MOVEMENT**—The way our bodies move effectively and efficiently while retaining perfect timing and balance.

2 **HOW THE BRAIN WORKS**—The basic functions of the brain and how it organises conscious and subconscious action.

3 **THE LEARNING ENVIRONMENT**—Creative learning and training situations which allow players to develop and hone their skills and cricketing temperament.

4 **ORGANISING YOURSELF FOR SUCCESS**—Maximising potential through good health, excellent physical and mental condition, situational awareness and good tactics, and personal development.

5 **LEADERSHIP**—Undertaking the leadership skills required for an effective team member, a good captain and an outstanding coach or administrator.

1

Each of these theories is expanded in its own chapter.

Have you ever seen those old films of Bradman batting, or more recently Glenn McGrath bowling, and how Ricky Ponting moves so brilliantly in the field? Have you noticed how relaxed and confident they are, how effortlessly they hit, bowl or field the ball, how beautifully balanced they are, and how consistent they are? They all comply with the five critical pathways to success. By making them the key concepts in your game, you should be able to maximise your skills, your confidence and temperament, and your understanding and appreciation of the sport. I'm not promising that you'll become another Bradman — I had enough trouble with that one myself — but I do believe you will improve and develop your game to your full potential.

A book for everyone

This book is designed for everyone: kids, enthusiasts, club cricketers, coaches, administrators and professional cricketers. The information in it is derived from fifty years of experience playing, watching and coaching the game: playing backyard test matches with my brothers Ian and Trevor when I was a kid growing up in Adelaide, through school, representing the states of South Australia and Queensland, as player and captain of Australia, as an Australian selector, as a broadcaster and as coach of my home state team.

A couple of years ago, the former Victorian batter Ian Frazer and I were talking about the things that make cricketers great. I was coaching the South Australian team at the time and I was concerned about the way coaches normally focus on players' faults and try to fix them. Ian and I talked about something radically different and fantastically positive. We thought, 'Why not look at the great players in the modern era of the game over the last fifty years, and see what they did right, see what they did in common, and implant those secrets into the up and coming players of today.'

So we got videos of about twenty of the top players over the years — players such as Bradman, Tendulkar, Gavaskar, Barry Richards, Vivian Richards, Graeme Pollock, Sobers, Ponting, McGrath, Marshall, Lillee, Hadlee and Warne. And we locked ourselves in a hotel room with a video player for two days to see if we could unlock the secrets of the best players in the world.

The results were astonishing — a real revelation to us. What we discovered was that all these great cricketers moved in a certain way.

FIRSTLY, they created a situation where they were always ready and poised for action.

SECONDLY, they moved their bodies in such a way that they hit, bowled and threw with power.

THIRDLY, their bodies were usually beautifully balanced.

And finally, they had wonderful timing – it was often perfect.

To our amazement we soon realised we were dealing with the natural laws of physics! We called them the core principles of movement, which is the first critical pathway to success.

We decided to set up a forum to discuss our revelations with cricketers everywhere, and what better place to do that than on the Internet. Ian became my partner in www.chappellway.com and we began posting our ideas for discussion. The response has been remarkable, to say the least. At the time of publishing this book, the website has been in existence for a little under two years. We have received over four million hits, posted fifty discussion papers from sports enthusiasts, academics and experts all over the world, and answered 2500 questions. Not one single contributor has questioned the core principles of movement theory.

It's time to tell you what the core principles of movement are:

- **UNWEIGHTING** — to gain an active neutral position;
- **COILING** — loading up to store power;
- **USING LEVERS** — for balanced mobile movement; and
- **TIMING.**

The five pathways to success

The core principles of movement

These are the keys that will unlock the skill mysteries of the game. No matter who you are or what type of physique you have, by following and mastering these core principles of movement you will have taken the first step on the pathway to playing at your full potential.

Although you need to be fit and have a good mental approach, physique doesn't matter too much in cricket. Look at Bradman — a short, wiry man of about 170 centimetres (5 feet 7 inches). Yet there's never been a batter who could get to the pitch of the ball better or, at the opposite end of the spectrum, handle a bouncer better (as he did during the bodyline series in 1931–32). Everyone has a different physical make-up.

For example, I could never hit the ball with the same blinding power as the champion West Indian Vivian Richards. He is super-stocky and muscly and I am tall and sinewy. Simply put, we are of very different builds. Viv was one of the most exciting and powerful hitters of the ball in the modern era, but I still made as many runs, hit plenty of fours and sixes and we ended with similar test averages. Viv used his body's raw power whereas I took a different approach using timing and a special mental technique I developed. I will tell you about this in chapter 4.

The same applies to the blinding pace of Shoaib Akhtar versus the controlled fast–medium bowling of Glenn McGrath. McGrath's body simply couldn't sustain bowling at Shoaib's pace, but McGrath is recognised as one of the world's greatest-ever fast bowlers. He uses accuracy and guile to snare his opponents instead of brutal speed. Think about it. Think about all those great cricketers with the 'wrong' physique. How could they be so good? The answer is that they have understood and used the core principles of movement to the maximum. The core principles work for everybody, no matter how tall, short, stocky or wiry you are.

How the brain works

Once you've understood the core principles of movement it's important to at least get a basic understanding of how your brain — your software as I like to call it — organises your thought and movement processes. Understanding how the brain works is the second critical pathway to success. Because it's such a complex organ, a detailed study of the brain would take many years. But a general understanding is important because it places all the critical pathways in context and explains how you think, react and learn the way you do. Personally, I find these extraordinarily complex processes of the brain absolutely fascinating; once I get started I can't stop reading about them.

The learning environment

The third critical pathway on the journey to cricket success is having a creative and supportive environment in which to learn and train. I grew up in Glenelg, a seaside suburb of Adelaide, playing cricket every day in the backyard, in the local park and (in summer) on the beach with my brothers Ian and Trevor, and our various friends from school and the local neighbourhood. Sometimes there would be so many of us we'd have a couple of teams! This was a great environment to learn in — it was fun, it was fiercely competitive and we played under all sorts of conditions. These are all very important aspects of learning the game. Think about these three points:

- **WHAT YOU DO NEEDS TO BE FUN.** If it's not, you won't want to do it and you'll never get a passion for it. And without passion you'll never be great at what you do.

- **COMPETITION IS A KEY FACTOR IN SPORT.** It's the element that makes sportspeople improve, go one better. Competition is not about winning at all costs, it's about a benchmark you have to reach if you're going to play successfully. It doesn't matter whether you're playing cricket in the backyard or a social game of tennis or golf, you have to be on a level with the other players to get the most out of it.

- **THE ABILITY TO PLAY UNDER VARIOUS CONDITIONS IS VERY IMPORTANT.** It is the hallmark of great cricketers. Look at Sachin Tendulkar — he makes runs everywhere. Look at Malcolm Marshall — he got wickets everywhere.

In our backyard Dad built us a turf wicket, so we had a pitch with a slightly slow, even bounce. In the park we would 'borrow' the family motor mower and mow a strip on the grass so we had a fast wicket. And on the beach we would play on the edge of the water where the tennis ball would grab into the sand

and bounce. Even the little kids could bowl bouncers that would whistle around our ears. Everywhere we played we would emulate the great cricketers of the day; we'd have our own test matches. It was a fantastic learning environment.

I'm concerned by the way cricket is so structured today. For the first one hundred years the game was completely unstructured, but since the late 1970s it has changed dramatically into a very structured sport. I'm not saying that change is not inevitable or that we don't need to change along with the times, but it seems to me there should be a blend of the two. It worries me that we could be creating something that we will look back on in ten years and regret.

Let's look at how learning and training are generally set up. For most kids it's a training session during the week then a match on the weekend. In the training sessions they're likely to get ten to fifteen minutes of batting, a bit of a bowl and a bit of catching practice. On the weekend, if they go out cheaply or bat down the list or are not one of the chosen bowlers, they're likely to spend most of their time in the outfield or sitting on the boundary line. It's not much fun, and they're not playing much cricket.

At the senior level, practice drills have taken over from what practice needs to be about, and that's building skills and confidence in the context of match conditions and match pressure.

I believe sessions in the practice nets are often not the most efficient way to learn. Sure, cricketers always need some remedial work and that's when the nets are ideal, but I believe coaches generally need to make sure they have creative training programs that offer fun and diversity, build confidence and teamwork, and simulate various match conditions.

If you don't have, or didn't grow up in, a positive learning and training environment, create one now and experience what it does for you and your game.

Organising yourself for success

The fourth critical pathway is organising yourself for success. All five pathways described in this book apply to any sport, and in fact your whole life.

Firstly, you need to master skills; secondly, you need to understand how the brain works; thirdly, you'll benefit from having a positive learning environment;

fourth, you've got to be prepared to develop as a person; and finally, you've got to be a responsible leader.

Even if you're not the boss there will usually be some people who look to you as an example. Organising yourself for success is about doing those things necessary to develop yourself personally so that when you add the other layers of skills, experiences and leadership you will be successful. For example, you need to:

- **HAVE A POSITIVE OUTLOOK AND BE CONFIDENT.** Negative people usually don't succeed.

- **BE ABLE TO FOCUS AND CONCENTRATE FOR LONG PERIODS.** Great cricketers concentrate for long periods and exclude all unnecessary distractions from what they are doing at the time.

- **BE HEALTHY.** Be concerned about your diet and generally look after yourself.

- **BE FIT.** In order to perform at your best and concentrate during long periods of physical activity, build your strength so you can be in peak condition.

- **BE TACTICALLY AWARE OF WHAT'S GOING ON AROUND YOU.**

- **BE ABLE TO REFLECT ON SITUATIONS** to find creative ways of doing what you want to achieve.

- **DEVELOP AS A PERSON OUTSIDE THE SPORT.** This way you'll find your cricket helps your life, and your life helps your cricket.

The top cricketers have very busy lives because not only do they play a lot of cricket, they are busy organising themselves for success.

When you think about it, these are all aspects of your personal development and are the same criteria you need to be successful in your life and career. One of the great things about cricket (and sport generally) is that it opens doors to other opportunities. You meet a lot of different people from all walks of life. If you play at the senior level, this is often seen as a benchmark for your life generally, and you gain a reputation for being successful.

Although professional cricket and other sports at the elite level are full-time occupations, there is always time to do other things. I used to read a lot — biographies of successful people and motivational books. When we weren't playing I would do courses and go to seminars; and I was fortunate to work for organisations such as AMP and Coca-Cola Bottlers, where I went through training programs in marketing and management. Today, with the Internet, it's so easy to find information – all sorts, ranging from nutrition and fitness to communications to the power of positive thinking. As well, most universities have distance education courses that you can complete on the Internet. You don't even have to leave home to get a degree! These are all things that relate to your personal development and I'm absolutely positive they feed back into your game and make you a better cricketer.

Leadership

Critical pathway five is leadership. As mentioned, leadership is a personal attribute that applies to everyone. It's an approach that you bring to your bowling, your batting, your fielding and your teamwork. You mightn't be the captain or the coach, but you may be a front-line bowler or one of the key fielders. You can bring leadership to those positions by setting an example in your training and on-field routines.

There is a common perception that leadership in cricket boils down to four positions: captain, vice-captain, coach and administrator. The best captains are good tacticians and communicators who understand and encourage their players. Good vice-captains offer invaluable support, whether it be tactics or helping the captain communicate with the rest of the team. The best coaches are nurturers and mentors, not autocrats. Good coaches set creative training programs. They identify the strengths in players and build on them, and they observe their players' problems and work with them to find solutions.

These days, with full-time coaches setting training programs and being so involved with team development, you could well ask: Where does coaching stop and captaincy begin? I like to define it this way. The coach works behind the scenes as a nurturer and a mentor, and setting the training and development programs. The captain is in charge of devising the game plan and the tactics used during the game. Of course, in good positive relationships the captain and coach would work together on the game plan and discuss tactics during the match, but from my point of view those are the basic parameters; come match day the captain is in charge.

In cricket the captain is more important than their counterpart in almost any other sport. In most sports, football for example, coaches take the leading role.

But cricket is one of the few games where the captain is the person who's the leader and that's an important and integral part of our game. On the field, split-second decisions by the captain can change the course of a match. Key tactics such as changing bowlers, field placing and building pressure on the opponent can mean the difference between winning and losing – and it can all happen very quickly. The captain is the one on hand who triggers the offensive (or defensive) move.

Coaching and leadership

In junior cricket, of course, the coach will naturally be the focus. But I still argue that even here nurturing and mentoring are the keys. For example, the coach can create situations that develop teamwork and team spirit, let the young players know what's expected of them and give them parameters and responsibilities. If the coach is the one making 100 per cent of the decisions then we're probably not going to educate too many future captains. I believe that captaincy and other responsibilities should be shared around at the junior level, otherwise we will just keep a whole lot of future cricketers out of the game.

Coaching is about creating a culture that extends through the various levels of cricket: club, state and national. And that's where Australia has stolen the march on the world of cricket over the last twenty years. We've got a structure in place where the players are being developed in a similar sort of style. Hopefully, within that structure, they're allowed the freedom to express their own individuality, to develop their own natural style and leave their own imprint and personality on the Australian team.

Cricket – the game

So for me cricket has been a journey. For every bit I put into this game I loved so much to play, I seemed to get some other opportunity in life in return. Through cricket I learnt about public relations, business and leadership. I learnt about staying healthy, being fit and being mentally alert. And I learnt about always trying to develop personally. That's what the game has been for me and just about everyone else I know.

If you master these five critical pathways to success, you are on your way to becoming a successful cricketer in the twentyfirst century.

CHAPTER 1

The Core Principles of Movement

*The four core principles of movement do not only apply to cricket,
they can be applied to every other ball sport as well: golf, tennis, football,
basketball, netball, hockey, anything.*

This chapter deals with cricket's fundamental skills. But look again at the table of contents at the beginning of this book. What, no forward defence? No square cut? No, none of that. Nor will I be telling you to do drills in the nets such as getting your dad or brother or best friend to throw balls well up outside the off stump a hundred times so you can practise your cover drive. I won't be suggesting you change your bowling style either, unless you look like injuring yourself. Why? Because those things are not the reasons why great cricketers are successful. Sure, they are beautiful stroke-players and have an excellent defence, and bowl a very controlled line and length, but what has made the great players technically brilliant is mastering the four principles of movement:

- UNWEIGHTING to create an active neutral position;
- COILING to store power;
- USING LEVERS for balanced mobile movement; and
- TIMING.

When I was coaching South Australia's state team, the Southern Redbacks, I often thought that cricket was a very difficult game to teach. Intuition told me that how well you learn the game depends on the quality of the environment in which you learn. I've watched coaches across the various states of Australia and in different countries. I've read countless books on sports coaching, been to dozens of conferences and listened to many experts on how to play cricket. And what has struck me is that the teaching of cricket is very ad hoc, with people plucking things out of the air that have little or no logic or purpose.

One of the problems is that coaches often try to coach feelings. But how the coach feels batting or bowling is probably very different to how the player feels in those same situations. I remember the first time I saw myself bat on television — it didn't look like it felt. Today, players use videotapes all the time to adjust their game. I'm glad I didn't; I might have changed things. So as a coach I kept asking myself the question: What should we be teaching?

Learning from the champions

I've always thought that when you want to learn something you should learn from the best — see how they do things. That's why, throughout my cricket career and ever since, I've been a prolific reader. I've always got half a dozen books on the go. Not fiction so much, but biographies of fascinating people who have dreams and achieve them, motivational books about successful businesspeople and people with great vision, and books about physical and mental well-being.

That was the kind of thinking behind Ian Frazer — the former Victorian batter and partner in my website (www.chappellway.com) — and I locking ourselves away in a hotel room for two days with videotapes of twenty-three great cricketers from the last 50 years. We wanted to see how the best guys did it.

As we sat there, analysing each batter's, bowler's and fielder's game, we began to see a pattern emerge. The first thing we noticed was that every single one of the batters was perfectly poised, ready to attack the ball. Then, when we looked at the bowlers it was the same — every bowler reached a point just prior to their delivery stride when their body was poised in the perfect state of readiness to bowl the ball. With fielding and wicket-keeping the same applied. Everyone was at this perfect point of readiness, *unweighted* and poised to strike. It didn't matter whether it was Sachin Tendulkar or Adam Gilchrist or me or Dennis Lillee or Shane Warne or Mutiah Muralitharan, each had their own way of getting ready.

THE GREAT CRICKETERS WE LEARNT FROM

Shoaib Akhtar	Sunil Gavaskar	Malcolm Marshall	Sir Garfield Sobers
Sir Donald Bradman	Adam Gilchrist	Muttiah Muralitharan	Sachin Tendulkar
Allan Border	Sir Richard Hadlee	Ricky Ponting	Shane Warne
Greg Chappell	Brian Lara	Graeme Pollock	Mark Waugh
Ian Chappell	Dennis Lillee	Barry Richards	Steve Waugh
Joel Garner	Rod Marsh	Sir Vivian Richards	

We called it *'unweighting — to create an active neutral position'*.

This was exciting. We couldn't wait to see if Barry Richards, Richard Hadlee and the others could give us more clues. They did.

The next thing we observed was the way they would get wound up like a spring with all this energy ready to explode. It didn't matter whether it was Rod Marsh behind the stumps, Barry Richards batting, Shoaib Akhtar bowling or Mark Waugh fielding, they had all rotated their body to store up energy ready for action.

Think about it. Grab a bat — a tennis racquet, golf club, anything. Get yourself ready to hit the ball. Now stop — just when you're coiled up ready to go through with your shot. Do you feel it? Try it again, this time picking up a ball and throwing. Now stop just before you actually throw. Can you feel the stored up energy?

We called it *'coiling — loading up to store power'*.

The lights were coming on! What next?

We looked at the movement stage of striking and releasing the ball. In batting, that's the back-lift, the movement of the feet and swing of the bat to make contact with the ball. In bowling it's loading up on the back leg, setting up the front leg and bringing the arm over to release the ball. We watched Shane Warne, Joel Garner and Garfield Sobers. We watched my brother Ian, Graeme Pollock and Ricky Ponting. And then we watched the greatest of them all — Don Bradman.

No matter what their physique — it didn't matter if they were tall, short, skinny or solid — each one moved their arms and legs into a position to retain perfect balance throughout the movement. Their bodies are lever systems.

We called it *'using levers — for balanced mobile movement'*.

Think about it. Get up from the chair where you're reading and try it for yourself. Notice when you are playing a shot how your arms and legs become levers. Now try bowling — same thing. Now try fielding and keeping — same thing.

Had we uncovered Don Bradman's secret?

There was still something missing, something incomplete. For although the movements we had identified made perfect sense, and each great cricketer completed those three movements, there was still the unanswered question of why one shot was hit more sweetly than another, or why some balls had that extra dynamic and other balls didn't.

We watched Tendulkar, Shoaib, Lillee, Gavaskar, Warne, Sobers — and finally it hit us when Ian asked me, almost in frustration, 'What is it that effects the timing?' I said, 'That's it! It's *timing*!'

That was the final element. It doesn't matter whether you're batting, bowling, fielding, catching, throwing or wicket-keeping, the *timing* of the movement is crucial. When it takes less than a second for the ball to travel the length of the pitch, about a quarter of a second for a snick to reach the keeper, timing is the difference between failure and success.

We were so knocked out we felt like Isaac Newton (1642–1727), the famous physicist and mathematician, when the apple fell on his head and led to him discovering the laws of gravity! And rightly so, because we soon realised that our first three principles of *unweighting*, *coiling* and *using levers* adhered to the laws of physics, and, to be precise, Newton's laws of motion: the law of inertia and gravity, the law of levers and force, and the law of action and reaction.

These are natural laws of physics, things that all of us on this planet have got to adhere to at every moment. We can't fight the laws of gravity, we can't fight the laws of force and acceleration, we can't fight the laws of levers because we're a lever system. So we borrowed our terminology from Newton and came up with unweighting, coiling and using levers.

The fourth principle, *timing* is also related to physics, but a different theory with a creator who's even more famous — Einstein. Albert Einstein (1879–1955) proposed that timing depends on the situation. For a batter, that's the bowler and the type of ball bowled, the atmosphere, the pitch and the fielders. For bowlers, keepers and fielders similar situations apply.

The upshot is that to maximise Einstein's timing you have to optimise Newton's laws: unweighting, coiling and using levers.

I said to Ian, 'How are we going to test this to make sure it's correct?' We decided to put it up on the website at chappellway to test the marketplace with these theories. Two years, four million hits and 20000 postings later no one has disagreed.

There are two points to be made about these principles that I find quite remarkable. First, they are simply how the body uses gravity and the laws of physics to move. They are completely natural. How simple and straightforward is that? In a game with such difficult skills as cricket, this was a real revelation to us. The second remarkable aspect is that these principles of movement can be applied to every other ball sport as well: golf, tennis, football, basketball, netball, hockey, you name it.

These four principles cannot be executed one at a time – they are one total, fluid movement regime. However, if they are examined separately, they are easier to explain and easier to understand.

Unweighting to gain an active neutral position

An object will always be at rest, or will not change its speed or direction unless it is acted upon by an outside, unbalanced force.
NEWTON'S FIRST LAW OF MOTION: THE LAW OF INERTIA

We all have inertia, and it's not just on Sunday mornings when we're lying in bed feeling lazy. Inertia is the quality that every person, animal and object has that makes them resist changes in their motion. Try this. Stand up with your feet a few centimetres apart. Without bending your legs, try to jump. How hard was that! I bet you got nowhere. Now bend your body and knees into a crouching position and try it again. How much better was that!

Why does this occur? As Newton's law says, an external force is needed to generate movement. This force is called the *ground reaction force*, which is simply the ground pushing back against your body, *unweighting* it. Your body uses gravity to crouch into position like a spring, then it unleashes its force, overriding gravity for a second or two while you're airborne. Gravity is the external force that assists in lowering the body, and the ground is the external force that initiates the acceleration of the movement upwards.

So unweighting is really about the laws of gravity. If you want to move, you have to access the ground forces and activate the right muscle groups to get motivated and get moving.

Here's a truism: all movement requires the body to unweight. Do we unweight to walk? The answer is 'yes'. If we're standing still we've got to lower our centre of gravity to load and unload one leg after the other to access the ground forces to move forward. Do we unweight to run? Absolutely. High jumpers unweight when they take off on their run-up and then again before they jump — just like bowlers do at the beginning of their run-up and into their delivery stride. Tennis players unweight when they are about to serve or waiting to receive. Think about it. When do footballers unweight in your favourite football code? For instance, a goalkeeper in soccer is standing on the goal line with the opposition player about to take a penalty kick. The goalkeeper lowers his centre of gravity and gets onto the balls of his feet so he can launch himself in whatever direction he needs to intercept the ball.

When Ian Frazer and I sat down to watch the videos of the best batters and bowlers of the past 50 years we saw a pattern begin to emerge. All but a few of them had exactly the same initial movement pattern. Sure, each had his own idiosyncratic way of doing it but the basic pattern was the same.

As the bowler loaded up for the delivery each batter levered the bat to a position close to parallel to the ground, toe of the bat pointing towards the slip cordon with the face slightly inclined to the off-side, arms relaxed and slightly bent. This action triggered by the top hand resulted in a shifting of the weight onto the ball of the back foot and inclined the body towards the bowler with the front foot hovering above the ground or slightly brushing the ground. It appeared to be a very active position, optimised for movement.

This was fascinating. Maybe we were onto something! What was it that caused all of these champion players to do the same thing? Then it occurred to us. They all must have had the same intention. If that was the case, then what was that intention? That too became obvious when we thought about it. They all intended to move toward the ball. How, you might ask, did we know that?

All movement patterns are organised by the unconscious brain. Once we intend to move in a certain direction, the brain automatically arranges the body so that the most efficient movements occur in an orderly, fluid fashion. If we change our mind about the direction in mid movement, the brain automatically makes the necessary adjustments. We do not have to think about each step in the chain.

The same process takes place when we are batting. Having an intention to move in one direction or the other is enough to trigger the brain to arrange the movements that are required to match the intention.

Try it for yourself. Stand with your weight evenly distributed on both feet with a magazine on the floor immediately to your left. Now move to step over the magazine to your left and observe what this intention triggers in the brain to allow this to happen. Now step back over the magazine to your right and observe once again.

What you should have noticed is that, as you intended to move to the left, the brain organised for a subtle shift of weight from the left foot onto the ball of the right foot with a slight bending of the right knee to allow you to push off to the left. The reverse will have happened as you went back to the starting position.

These same actions are taking place unconsciously all day long whether you are walking, gardening, stepping over puddles or playing sport. Your intention to move is enough to trigger the brain into action. You do not have to control each movement. In fact if you are thinking about each action you will actually interfere with the process.

So why do the best batters intend to move forward rather than prepare to play back? Wouldn't it be just as efficient to prepare to play back? The answer is an emphatic no!

Why it works best to intend to play forward until you are forced back is because the first point of release from the bowler's hand will be a full-pitched ball. If you prepare for the full ball you will still have time to adjust and push back if the ball stays in the hand longer and is short. In fact, the subconscious brain will begin to adjust before you are consciously aware that the ball will be short.

If you prepare for the short ball first you will not have enough time to adjust if the ball comes out of the hand early. In fact, you will most probably miss the ball coming out of the hand because the brain will be focussing on the expected later point of release.

This then is the secret of the champions.

If, as coaches, we can encourage this mind set in our players, this movement pattern will occur naturally. What a player thinks about will decide how efficient the movement patterns are, so the correct thought processes are critical to a player's chance of success. This is why as coaches we cannot afford to cause our players to be focused on their own movements. They must be focused on the ball with a clear intention to play forward and let the brain do the rest.

In cricket, whether you're batting, bowling or fielding, you need to organise yourself to unweight at precisely the right moment. It's crucial for quality movement.

Unweighting for batting

For batting, there are two things to unweight: the body and the bat. Both are critical.

When I'm batting, my instinct always tells me to move before the bowler has bowled. It's a psychological thing. I face up and I think: 'Well, I better get moving to give myself more time.' But a lot of the movements we make at this point are wrong. If you commit yourself to a significant move forward before the ball is bowled and it turns out to be short, you're in trouble, because you can't go back. If the ball is pitched up, but not quite full enough, and you've already committed your weight onto the front foot, it may be in the wrong position — and you can't reposition yourself unless you get the weight off it and start again. And there's not time for that.

UNWEIGHTING THE BAT AND THE BACK-LIFT

The commonly used term *back-lift* is often misunderstood. The inference is that the bat should be lifted to initiate the action, whereas in fact the initial movement should be nothing more than a semi wrist-cock. Basically, this initial movement is a continuation of the bat tap that most batters naturally do as the bowler approaches. The semi wrist-cock is part of the unweighting process of the body and the bat. Many players mistakenly think of the back-lift as one continuous movement, whereas it is in fact two distinct movements (albeit the separation in the two movements is almost indistinguishable, particularly when playing an attacking shot). The first part of the movement is the unweighting process of both body and bat where we aim to achieve the active neutral position in preparation to respond to the ball. The critical part of this wrist-cock is that it must be initiated by the top hand. Many of the problems of batting can be related back to the incorrect initiation using the bottom hand with its implications on balance and the down-swing of the bat.

My instinctive feeling to want to get moving before the bowler has bowled is correct, but only as long as I'm doing the right things, and that is to *unweight the body* and *unweight the bat*. We've all seen batters tap the bat on the ground as the bowler comes into bowl — that's unweighting the bat. But there's a right way and a wrong way to do it.

It's very important that the unweighting of the bat is initiated with the top hand. Here's how you do it. You can practise doing this with a lighter instrument such as a tennis racquet or cricket stump using only your top hand. You should notice the flexing of the elbow but importantly notice how it locks in the muscle groups around the front shoulder that will lead into the body coil. Check the pictures and try it out.

Standing at the crease, unweighting the bat. Notice how it is unweighted towards second slip.

Unweighting the bat: the top hand initiates the wrist-cocking movement while the thumb and forefinger of the bottom hand act as a fulcrum.

Bats are heavy objects, especially if you let them hang, and even heavier when you are trying to move them. Even small objects are heavy if you don't hold them properly. Try holding a bottle of mineral water and letting it hang like a bat. Notice how heavy it is? If you're facing the bowler with your bat hanging, it's a lot heavier than a bottle, and it means you've got a lot of muscles in use that will need to be released before you can use them again. But by unweighting the bat using the lever technique, you need much less muscle power, and your muscles are relaxed and ready for the main game.

Unweighting the bat this way also causes another positive movement. It locks the front shoulder in the correct position: left shoulder for a right-hander, right shoulder for a left-hander. This now enables you to take the shoulder in the direction you want the ball to go.

If you pick the bat up with the bottom hand it locks the *back* shoulder in, leaving the front arm and shoulder loose. This creates two problems. One, it will shift your weight over the back foot, which takes you back into a weighted position from which it is difficult to recover. Two, your back shoulder leads you into the shot, which means your body spins out prematurely and your bat will go across the line. Your whole body must open up to allow the bat to come back into the ball. For example, you might be wanting to hit a front foot drive through the covers, but your shoulders will be pointing to wide mid-on, and you'll be forced to fall away to the off side while your lower body tries to retain balance through the hit.

> ### KIDS AND HEAVY BATS — A BIG NO-NO!
>
> A lot of young players pick their bat up with their bottom hand instead of unweighting it because the bat is too heavy for them. What happens is that the brain registers that the bat is too heavy and tells the batter, 'Pick it up with the bottom hand.' Be careful, especially when you're young or have a light physique, not to use a heavy bat. It's a real handicap.

There's another problem that occurs if you activate the shot with your bottom hand. I'm a right-hander and as my weight shifts away to the right-hand side of my body I can feel my weight going down through the heel of my back foot to support me and keep balance. If you activate the shot with the top hand, your hands remain within the perimeter of your feet, so you keep control of the lower body during the unweighting movement. By unweighting the bat with the top hand, everything is locked in correctly. Now you are perfectly positioned to react appropriately to the delivery. You'll find that the bat loads

Unweighting the bat correctly allows you to play through the line of the ball.

Unweighting the bat wrongly causes your back shoulder to lead you into the shot.
Your body rotates out prematurely causing you to play across the line.

properly from the top of your back-lift all the way through the down-swing and into the ball.

Unweighting your body is the other crucial thing you need to do in preparing yourself for batting action. This allows you to get your body into an active neutral position so that once the ball is bowled you can quickly move into the best position to play the shot. To unweight the body, you need to lower the centre of gravity by doing two things:

1 flex the knees;

2 bring your weight onto the ball of your back foot so that you are in a position to go towards the ball.

This loads the back foot, and from this position you can ultimately push forward, push back, go sideways, adjust, duck and weave — in fact go in any direction you want.

The critical point here is that the weight must be on the ball of the foot. If the weight goes down on the heel again it becomes a weighted position from which it is difficult to recover. If, on the other hand, you commit yourself significantly *forward* before the ball is bowled, you will be assuming another weighted position that reduces your options. By planting the front foot you'll commit yourself to delivering the bat.

The critical point to remember is that by making any significant heel strike in your first movement, that is, if your heel takes any real weight on the ground, that foot will have to be unweighted again to move further. If, however, you unweight the body appropriately you can project yourself forward or back (or wherever) to set up an appropriate position.

This is why Bradman had the greatest range, even for a man who was only 170 centimetres tall. He had an enormous stride because he created the perfect unweighted position. This allowed him to maximise the distance he could accelerate his bat through the shot, a characteristic of all the very best players.

Best position

So, to take you back to the point I made about intuition always telling me to move as the bowler is running in, unweighting solves that problem and gets you into perfect readiness to play your shots. The next time you're at the cricket or watching on television, take a look at the top batters. See how they move on the crease while they are waiting for the bowler as he runs in to

Unweighting the body and bat. Notice in this sequence of photographs how the body looks balanced, relaxed and ready to pounce.

deliver the ball. As the bowler got into his delivery stride I would prepare to move towards the ball by loading my back foot. By preparing to move forward to as many balls as possible I was putting myself in the best position to deal with whatever delivery I received.

Unweighting also helps you to relax your upper body and allows it to prepare for the job it's about to do. This is very important because if your upper body is tense it drives the weight down into your feet, causing too much heel contact with the ground. Once this happens, you can't unweight your feet easily anymore and most of your movement options to play the ball are closed down.

So if we bring the unweighting of the bat and the unweighting of the body together — that's the tapping of the bat and slight movement onto the ball of the back foot at the crease — we can be in perfect readiness to play our shots. And that's what it's all about — playing shots to score runs.

UNWEIGHTING — TWO FACTS

- If you make a commitment to plant the front foot or back foot before the ball is bowled, you will have reduced your options and the ability to respond by 50 to 80 per cent.

- With an unweighted body and unweighted bat you are in a position to respond 100 per cent to anything the bowler delivers; you can go in any direction you want to.

Let me take you through what happens in this scenario. As you tap your bat, you unweight it by initiating the movement with your top hand. Your bottom hand is nice and loose with essentially only your thumb and forefinger (or the tips of the bottom-hand fingers) in contact with the bat. The toe of the bat points in the direction of first or second slip. This locks in the front shoulder.

Next, flexing your knees slightly, you move your weight onto the ball of your back foot. At this stage the ball is bowled. As you decide whether you're going to play forward or back, your arms and bat will load (back-lift) according to the direction and power of the hit. If you decide to play a cover drive, for example, you will start to take a big stride forward. The natural counterbalancing action of the body will then force you to shift your arms and the weight of the bat backwards, behind your back foot. You are moving into position, and at the same time creating the body coil to store the energy that you will unleash to play the shot.

Now you can see why you don't want any excessive back-lift before the ball is bowled: until you've decided what sort of ball it is, you don't want to get yourself out of balance. So, unweighting like this really gives you an added benefit — it stops you from committing yourself before the ball is bowled. It's like a boxer who's dancing around in the ring. He's got his hands in close to the body and he's ready to be able to respond to what he sees from his opponent. If his weight is on his heels, it's not going to be long before his weight is on his bum, because he'll be flat on his back. But the boxer in the unweighted position can brace, take punches, give punches, and duck and weave to avoid punches.

UNWEIGHTING FOR BATTING

Unweighting is finding that active *neutral position*, a position of alertness, where you are ready to spring, ready to respond to what the bowler has bowled, and ready to unleash all your energy into the shot. You are in a position where you have all options open to you.

You've satisfied:

- the psychological need to get moving before the ball is bowled —this relaxes you and gives you more time;

- the laws of gravity and the laws of motion — you've lowered your centre of gravity so you can access the ground force to be ready for rapid movement in any direction.

Not every good batter unweights efficiently. I can think of two – both were good players for England. One was Graham Gooch and the other was Tony Greig. Both used to face up standing upright and holding their bat away from their body. It was not a good starting point. However, both were gifted players.

If you study Gooch's stance more closely you will find that, although he faced up with his weight over his back foot, as the ball was bowled he leant forward onto his front foot to get the unweighting he needed to be able to load his back foot ready to push off. This action tended to create an inordinate amount of weight on his front foot, but by going down through the *ball* of the foot he was able to get away with it. If his weight had stayed on his back leg, he could never have gone back and he would have struggled to go very far forward; and if he had moved onto the *heel* of his front foot he would never have moved any-where. It was far from perfect, but it was unweighting nevertheless and it shows that heel strike is very important.

Throughout his career my brother Ian had quite a pronounced backwards movement as the ball was about to be delivered. So did Steve Waugh when he started. But the thing that saved Ian is that his back heel didn't make a significant strike on the ground, so he could still go forward or further back. Steve struggled early in his career against fast bowlers because he often made a significant heel strike. He made some adjustments later in his career and became much more effective in his unweighting, which increased his options.

UNWEIGHTING is why the good players look so good: they're in a position to respond immediately and efficiently to what they see as the ball leaves the bowler's hand. So if we're going to teach young batters anything, let's teach them to unweight correctly. Unweight the body, unweight the bat, make it nice and relaxed so you are poised in the perfect position to make the shot.

Unweighting for bowling

Unweighting for bowling is just as crucial as it is for batting.

Take the example of the high jumper I mentioned earlier. Most high jumpers measure out a run-up. It's systemised and gets them to a point — the launch point. A critical factor for high jumpers is that they land on the ball of the foot on their take-off leg. This enables them to lower their centre of gravity and access the ground forces in order to launch themselves upwards.

It's very much the same with bowlers in cricket. They also have a carefully measured run up which culminates at a 'landing spot' close to the bowling crease. They also land on the ball of the back foot so that they can push themselves up and over the front leg, which then lands. The bowler's weight is then transferred onto the front leg to bowl the ball. For right handers, the 'landing leg' is the right leg; for left handers it's the left leg.

Take a look at the pictures and then try it in slow motion to feel how it works because understanding unweighting for bowling is a critical factor in bowling success.

If the high jumper and the bowler land on the heel of their take-off leg into the jump they break the momentum gained from the run-up and their weight will go backwards and/or sideways, affecting their ability to unweight and coil.

Jason Gillespie is a good case in point when it comes to discussing unweighting for bowling. In my opinion Jason is close to the best fast bowler of his time, yet

Unweighting for bowling — the run-up. Notice how relaxed the body is and how much drive is generated through contact with the ground. The efficient use of the arms is also critical because of the effect it has on the unweighting of the legs. Each time an arm goes forward (the drive arm) in the running motion it will effect the unweighting efficiency of the opposite leg (action/reaction).

he had a real problem when I first started coaching South Australia. He was getting a lot of leg injuries, an ongoing issue for him.

For bowlers to unweight correctly, they need to land on the ball of their foot. The force of landing results in just a touch of stabilising heel strike. As they unweight, their centre of gravity is naturally lowered. Jason's problem was that he was travelling too fast to unweight efficiently, which caused instability in his delivery stride.

But let's hear it from Jason himself.

> *My run-up was very long and very fast, and I was hitting the crease with too much forward momentum. It was really getting me in the legs, they weren't strong enough to sustain the force my run-up and delivery landing was putting on them and I was having injury after injury. Not only that, I'd bowl a good ball then I'd bowl a bad ball, so my consistency was affected. One day Greg said to me, 'Mate, you know you've got to think about shortening your run-up because you don't want to be hitting the crease so hard that you can't control your back foot landing position.' He pointed out that when I landed on my back leg,*

I was so far up on the ball of my foot, and coming in so hard at the crease, that my heel was swivelling about ninety degrees and this was making my whole body very unstable.

Jason's leg — his knees, ankles, everything — were under a huge amount of stress and a lot of that pressure was being transferred to his back. This meant he had no stability.

A critical aspect of unweighting for bowling is stability, particularly if it effects spinal integrity at either back-foot or front-foot landing in the delivery stride. If your back foot starts swivelling as you are trying to unweight, your uncoiling is compromised. This means your spine is twisting as you land on your back leg and this puts incredible pressure on your back because you are off-balance. Jason was having exactly these problems with the rotation of his leg and the integrity

Unweighting for bowling actually has two 'unweighting moments'. The first is the take-off stride, which is the penultimate step leading to the jump. The bowling arm is critical to the proper unweighting and loading of the body at this stage. As with the top hand in batting, the bowling arm sets up the ideal chain reaction. If done incorrectly it will impede the ability to coil the body.

The second 'unweighting moment' is when the back foot lands. If the unweighting and coiling of the body has been done properly into the penultimate stride this should flow automatically to the back foot landing, generating more momentum to complete the delivery.

of his spine. So the first thing we discussed was shortening his run-up so he could have more control at this point. He was always going to land high up on the ball of his foot — he could never change that — but at least he could take measures to control the swivelling action when his back foot landed. He was really worried about it and I remember him saying to me, 'Oh, but I want to be a fast bowler.' And I replied, 'You'll always be a fast bowler because you're designed to bowl fast. But what we've got to do is to make sure that you can do it more consistently with more control.' So we set out to do just two things which I believed would solve his problems:

- shorten his run-up to make it much more measured and precise;

- work on the efficiency of his run-up so that his momentum was optimal at the point of delivery, meaning that his momentum was under control rather than out of control.

The results were startling, to say the least, and they're in the scorebook for every cricket fan to see. By being under control in his unweighting he could now bowl the ball wherever he wanted. The rotational effect on landing from the longer run had not only made him susceptible to injury, it caused instability in his delivery action which in turn caused problems with his control and direction. His fluctuation in pace was now minimal, whereas before he'd bowl some really fast balls and suddenly two or three balls that were 10 kilometres per hour slower with less control. Now there was only a two or three kilometre per hour range in every ball that he bowled. It was not only a great result for Jason, it was a great result for me as a coach, because it showed the sort of things the coach can do to help their players: just being aware of what they are doing, helping them with problems and working with them on ways of improving their game.

So the integrity of your spine is critical at two points: when you land on your back leg, and again when you land on the front foot of your delivery stride. If you follow this rule you should bowl with a lot more control and be free of back problems, unless there are other structural issues that contribute.

Spin bowlers

Of course, the same rules apply to spin bowling. Spin bowlers have to use their unweighting differently from fast bowlers who gain more momentum from their run-up. Because their run-up is shorter spin bowlers need to be

The unstable landing leg. It swivels causing instability, problems with control and direction, and susceptibility to injury.

The stable landing leg. Promotes better stability and therefore better timing overall, better control and direction, and less susceptibility to injury.

more efficient in their use of the ground forces that they generate from their run-up. The penultimate step is critical in establishing enough force to efficiently transfer the momentum into the body coil just prior to the back foot landing and, in turn, to allow the body time to unwind optimally through delivery.

This series of photographs shows Shane Warne unweighting.

A great start for good sustained bowling that doesn't over stress your body is unweighting properly just prior to the point of delivery. Land on the ball of your foot on your back leg. The force of landing results in just a touch of stabilising heel strike. Now you can access the ground forces that drive you up and over to complete the delivery action.

Unweighting for fielding

When we were looking through the tapes of all the famous players, Ian Frazer and I came across a great piece of footage. Sachin Tendulkar was batting, Shane Warne was bowling, Adam Gilchrist was the keeper and Mark Waugh was at first slip. What a collection of players! They all had their eyes firmly fixed on Warnie as he commenced his run-up. And then, as he got into his delivery stride, you could see Tendulkar unweight, Gilchrist unweight and Waugh unweight. All three of them unweighted simultaneously. They were all like tigers ready to pounce.

The point is that unweighting is just as crucial for fielding and wicket-keeping as it is for batting and bowling. Take the example of slips fielders. Let's say that instead of them crouching down like they normally do they were standing up stiff and straight. What would happen if the ball came to them? They would be very lucky to catch it because firstly, they would have to unweight in order to move, and then secondly, they would have to make the appropriate move to catch it. By that time the ball would be halfway to the boundary.

So what do the great slips fielders do — guys like Bobby Simpson, Mark Waugh and Ian Chappell? As the bowler is running in they stand with their hands on their knees. Then, as the bowler gets into their delivery stride they get into their unweighted position.

When I was fielding in the slips the first thing I'd do is watch the bowler in his run-up and delivery stride — unweighting of course. Then I'd concentrate hard on the ball as it came out of his hand so I would get an indication of where it was going to go — whether it was short, full, wide, outside leg stump, or outside off stump. If it was outside leg stump I would be thinking that I wouldn't be in this play at all. But I would still be ready for it — the batter might get a top edge to a short ball or a leading edge to a drive. So I'd probably be leaning, ready to run towards the leg side if I had to. But if I saw the ball pitched well up outside off stump, then I'd be getting ready for it.

And what I learnt through experience was two things:

- If the ball was well up, the catches would probably be from waist height down.

- If the ball was short, the catches would probably be from waist height up.

So, while I was unweighting, if I saw that the ball was well pitched up, I would stay low. But if it was short I'd get myself ready to come up. Experience is very important; I discuss it more in 'Training and practice' in chapter 3. It gives you the advantage of being able to predict things a little bit.

The 'height rule' applies to both fast bowling and spin. If it's well up and the batter is playing forward, the snick will most likely be low. But if the ball is short snicks are mostly going to come from cut shots; not only will they probably come high and a little faster, they might also go wide. So, as well as unweighting, I'd be ready to back off towards third man. Sometimes anticipating the ball in this way can get you in to trouble, for instance, it could fly between you and the keeper. But that's unusual, and usually the keeper is moving across as well, so the gap is covered.

TEN GREAT SLIPS FIELDERS

Ian Botham	Ricky Ponting	Mark Taylor
Tony Greig	Viv Richards	Mark Waugh
Ian Chappell	Bob Simpson	
Clive Lloyd	Garfield Sobers	

Another thing I learnt from experience was that when fielding at second or third slip, I tended to watch the batter more than the bowler. This is simply because I had shifted away from the line of the ball to a more side-on position, so I would just watch the bowler out of the corner of my eye and get an indication of length more than anything else, rather than line. Again, if I saw it was short the potential catch would probably be up around chest height, but if it was well pitched up I'd be ready to catch it a bit lower.

To put it another way, if I saw the batter launching into a drive then I knew catches would probably be low. But if I saw the batter launching into a cut shot then I knew that the ball would fly differently and would probably be more likely to come at me waist high or higher.

These are the things you learn from experience, but they all start with correct unweighting.

Of course, all fielders should get themselves into that active neutral position as the bowler is about to deliver the ball. Fielders who are not close to the bat, and outfielders, should take a few paces in — that's also unweighting. But when you're taking those few paces make sure they're not too fast, because if they are you can build up too much momentum and can be caught between strides when the ball is hit to you. You have to be poised in that active neutral position, ready to go every which way.

My advice is to concentrate on the batter and try to anticipate where they are going hit the ball, so that you're in a position where you've got all your options open to you when the ball is hit. It's very important that when you're fielding away from the bat you take your cues from the batter.

TEN GREAT OUTFIELDERS FROM THE LAST FIFTY YEARS

Colin Bland	Javed Miandad	Doug Walters
Allan Border	Norman O'Neil	Mark Waugh
Neil Harvey	Ricky Ponting	
Clive Lloyd	Viv Richards	

TEN GREAT WICKET-KEEPERS FROM THE LAST FIFTY YEARS

Wasim Bari	Wally Grout	Syed Kirmani
Jeffrey Dujon	Ian Healy	Derek Murray
Godfrey Evans	Alan Knott	
Adam Gilchrist	Rod Marsh	

I used to just love going to the cricket and watching good fielders — guys like Bobby Simpson, Neil Harvey and Norm O'Neil. And it was fantastic being on the field with great fielders like Ian Botham, Tony Greig and my brother Ian Chappell — not so great if you snicked one to them, though. In recent years I loved going to watch Mark Waugh, and I often wondered whether people really appreciated how good he was. He made fielding look so easy that most people didn't realise how difficult the piece of fielding or catch really was. He'd just catch them and throw them away and you'd think, 'That was easy'. But I knew from experience that it wasn't easy at all, and I don't think he got the credit for how good a fielder and how good a catcher he really was.

It was particularly interesting watching him field in close to the wicket in one-day games or test matches, particularly in Sydney where the wicket was really dusty and the ground was very uneven. I'd see blokes smash the ball at him and he'd just move to his left and scoop it up on the first bounce, and flick it away as though nothing had happened. The thing that used to amaze me was that he always got it in the middle of the hand, and because he made it look so effortless, no one budged. But I wanted to give him a standing ovation! It was simply awesome.

Ricky Ponting is a sensational fielder. Allan Border at forward square leg — some of his catching and throwing at the stumps was sensational. The English player, Derek Randall and the South African Jonty Rhodes did some spectacular things now and again. But they were almost too mobile — they actually made it look more spectacular than it really was, simply because they were moving in too fast, unweighting the wrong way. What makes Ricky Ponting so good is that he moves low to the ground; he's like a cat. He's a much better fielder than Jonty because he makes the difficult things look easy and he is more consistently effective.

It's very important for young kids, for everybody, when you go to the cricket or watch it on television, turn the volume down or cut out the chatter and actually watch the nuances of fielding, batting and bowling. The tendency is, and I've done it myself watching at home, you get really lazy and you don't really watch the cricket. You listen to what the commentators are telling you and when someone gets out or there's a close call, you sit up and watch the replay to get all the action. So it makes you a lazy watcher. Be a busy spectator and watch what the best fielders do.

Coiling to store power

Force = Mass x Acceleration
NEWTON'S SECOND LAW OF MOTION

Isaac Newton's second law of motion focuses on force. Essentially, it says that given an object with a constant mass (weight), the greater the acceleration, the greater the force. Force is measured in newtons, mass in kilograms and acceleration in metres per second squared (m/s^2). As human beings our mass is

Coiling for the pull shot. Notice how the hips are facing mid-on, but the top part of the body and shoulders are 'wound up' and facing mid-off, ready to transfer the built-up energy through the arms and bat to the ball.

more or less constant, so in order to generate force we have to accelerate. We do this by winding up, or 'coiling', like a spring. So Newton's second law explains why adults can create more force than kids – adults are heavier and have stronger muscles, that is, stronger 'springs'.

In cricket, when we 'coil' we use Newton's second law as it applies to human movement. Coiling is how we create torque (rotational force) which gives us power — power to hit the ball hard, to bowl fast, to put a lot of spin on the ball, or to throw in from the outfield. At the beginning of this chapter we discussed what it felt like just before you hit or threw a ball. There was all this stored up energy. That's Newton's second law ('coiling') at work.

Coiling creates the 'separation' of the shoulders and the hips. If your hips and shoulders are pointing in the same direction there's no coiling and therefore little stored up energy. But if you coil, that is 'twist' your shoulders so they are at (say) 60 degrees to your hips, you've created energy in your upper body that you can unleash through the torso. When you're batting that energy travels down through your arms, hands and fingers to the bat, which strikes the ball. If you're bowling or throwing, it's a similar dynamic, but this time the energy ends up in the projectile, the ball. Try it — that's the best way to see what I mean.

Let's take the pull shot as an example. The hips stay facing mid-on, but the top half of the body is coiled with the shoulders pointing pretty much towards mid-off, ready to unleash the energy to hit the ball. It's the same with the golf swing; the coiling of the body that creates the tension (the energy) that you then unleash through the club onto the ball. Tennis is the same too. You coil your shoulders back further than your hips to build up power to hit the ball. In batting, coiling is initiated on your back-lift. This is the part of the batting movement that creates the power.

The use of coiling is adjusted in batting to the demands of the situation. For example, the coil is restricted in defensive shots, the late cut and the leg glance, but there is a fully loaded coil with all the attacking shots like the drives, the pull and hook, and the square cut.

THE STRAIGHT BACK-LIFT — ONE OF THE WORST MISTAKES A BATSMAN CAN MAKE

The straight back-lift is one of the great myths of cricket, even if you want to hit straight. In fact, by moving the bat straight back you tend to activate the chest and upper arm muscles, which in turn make your movement very stilted and stiff. Try it. Your upper body is already prematurely coiled without having moved your hips.

In contrast, when you unweight the bat the correct way, using levers with the back-lift towards first or second slip, your leading shoulder will be nicely locked in and the laws of physics will do the rest for you. Once you get into your back-lift (the coil) the weight of the bat will drop in behind your hands, so whatever direction you start to go with your hands the weight of the bat will go in the same direction. This will bring the bat into the correct line from the peak of your back-lift to allow the hips to rotate and the bat to set itself in the direction of the shot. This is the natural physics of how the body plays through the line of the ball.

There's another problem caused by the straight back-lift — it makes it very hard to access balls on the middle and leg stumps because your body is in the way. Try it — you'll see what I mean. Your bat has to get around your body, making it virtually impossible to play effective on-drives and shots out through mid-wicket. The best you'll be able to do is *push* the ball.

In bowling and throwing, just as in batting, the upper body separates from the hips to create the coiling effect. In the jump the bowler rotates his shoulder to create a 'wound up spring' using the core muscles, those of the stomach and lower back. Like the back-lift, where the action is initiated by the top hand, this action is initiated by the bowling arm, which triggers the jump and loading of the top half of the body. Fast bowlers create a kind of slingshot using the shoulders and arm which transfers the energy through to the ball to make it go fast, whereas with slow bowlers a lot of the energy is transferred to the fingers to spin the ball. They need spin, not speed. In fielding, coiling is often very pronounced. In the outfield, when you chase a ball and field it, you're often in a position where your back is almost facing the direction in which you're throwing. This is because you have to create a lot of stored up power to throw the ball 80 metres with a nice flat trajectory over the stumps.

Left: Jeff Thomson is perhaps the most famous example of a fast bowler coiling. See how his upper body is 'wound up', with his arm right the way around his back ready to whip over like a sling shot.

Centre: Shane Warne coils during the delivery stride. Note the amount of energy he has built up through his body coil to put that deadly spin on the ball.

Right: Coiling for a long throw from outfield. Notice how the upper part of the body is virtually 'unleashed' from the hips.

Using levers for balanced mobile movement

For every action there is an equal an opposite reaction.
NEWTON'S THIRD LAW OF MOTION

Force always occurs in pairs, for example, action and reaction. Consider an athlete on the starting blocks. When the start gun goes 'bang' the athlete pushes back and down on the blocks, and in return the blocks push the athlete forward and upwards. The same law of physics applies in cricket where we use the body's natural 'levers', the arms and the legs, to shift the body's mass for the action and reaction to occur.

Look at these photographs. They are examples of levers for balanced mobile movement, as well as coiling.

Check out the shot of the famous Australian batter of the early 1900s, Victor Trumper, jumping down the wicket to drive. Victor was the first superstar of Australian cricket and this is one of the most extraordinary cricket photographs of all time. Look how perfectly balanced he is. Notice that his front leg is extended down the pitch and, to counterbalance that, his arms and bat are extended out way behind his body, with his back leg acting as a fulcrum. The fulcrum is the support from which the levers extend to counterbalance each other. And notice the coiling. You can see the creases in his shirt above the waistline and that his shoulders are turned about thirty to forty-five degrees to his hips.

Now check out the shot of the great English fast bowler of the 1950s, Frank 'Typhoon' Tyson, about to release the ball. Again, he is perfectly balanced using his arms and legs as levers. Notice too the energy he has built up through

Left: Victor Trumper jumping out to drive. *Right:* Frank 'Typhoon' Tyson about to let one rip.

coiling his upper body. In a split second that energy will be transferred to the ball to become blinding speed.

The coiling and levers movements are very closely related. In batting, apart from being critical to unweighting, the back-lift is involved in coiling and levers.

With a bat, face up as if you were going to play a ball. Now, without moving your legs, launch your bat into a back-lift as if you were going to do a cover drive off the front foot. I bet you nearly overbalanced. Now try the same thing, only with a forcing shot off the back foot. Go up on your toes and lift your bat back without moving your back foot. I bet you fell on your stumps this time. If you don't move that leg back to compensate for the weight of your bat now that it's away from your body, you overbalance.

In bowling it is exactly the same. Try bowling without raising your non-bowling arm to counterbalance your bowling arm. Now bowl without moving your front leg. What did you find? You become unbalanced and awkward, and create little or no power. This is all part of the natural action/reaction law.

Left: Dennis Lillee was considered a classic side-on bowler. Note how his landing back foot is side-on to the direction he's bowling to, and his arms and legs (his levers) are fully extended.

Centre: The great West Indian bowler, Malcolm Marshall, regarded as a front-on bowler, establishes a coiled position similar to Dennis at back-foot landing.

Right: Glenn McGrath is one of the most accurate bowlers the world has ever seen. Notice how his back-foot landing position is somewhere between Dennis Lillee's and Malcolm Marshall's.

COILING AND LEVERS FOR BOWLING

The similarity between all three of these bowlers is the degree of separation between shoulders and hips in the coiling phase. Their back-foot landing position is a result of each of them optimising this critical shoulder and hip separation.

SIDE-ON BOWLER

As the top hand triggers the unweighting and coiling in batting, the bowling arm triggers the unweighting and coiling in bowling. Having triggered the jump in the unweighting process it now triggers the coiling of the upper body as it travels back towards the centre line of the body. The action/reaction of the bowling arm causes the front shoulder to rotate, in turn causing the hips to rotate. As the hips complete their rotation, the back foot lands. Meanwhile, the upper body has started its uncoiling in preparation for delivery. Dennis Lillee was a great example of a side-on bowler. Jeff Thomson was a unique example of a side-on bowler. He would shuffle up to the wicket, hide his bowling hand behind his back, and then let it go with an enormous slingshot action. It was probably the most efficient side-on action ever seen, but it was only Jeff's incredible strength and flexibility that allowed him to coil over such a long distance.

FRONT-ON BOWLER

Front-on bowlers land with the back foot facing the batter. Malcolm Marshall was a great example of a front-on bowler. Malcolm would load up differently. Because of his strength and flexibility, he was able to create an extraordinary separation between his shoulders and hips in the jump. His back-foot landing position was required to allow him to uncoil rapidly. Consequently, his levers (arms and legs) had to stay shorter because he loaded up (coiled) over a shorter distance. He didn't have the big long arms (levers) that Dennis had, so he generated his pace from very quick arm action. In a way Malcolm was like Jeff Thomson. It was only their incredible strength and flexibility that allowed them to bowl as they did.

PARTIALLY OPEN

Bowlers like Brett Lee and Glen McGrath are a mixture of side-on and front-on. They tend to be a little more front-on with their back-foot landing direction than Dennis, but not as extreme as Malcolm. Again, the key is that they optimise their coil, allowing them all to assume loaded body positions into the back-foot landing.

Balance

By understanding how your body operates on levers, you can then take the next step of aiming for perfect balance. Sir Donald Bradman was the best batter ever to play the game because he was the best-balanced batsman ever to have played the game. I have only ever seen film footage of him playing but it's obvious from the limited footage available that his balance was exceptional. Even though he was a small man he was able to cover enormous distances forward and back because of this.

I have been fortunate enough to see the best batsmen since the early 1950s and they all have one thing in common: incredible balance. Balance is inherent in all of us, otherwise we would not be able to stay upright. Elite athletes may be blessed with more of it than the average person but much of it is learnt from hours and hours of practising specific skills.

The biggest impediment to balance for most batters is a psychological need to be moving before the ball is bowled. It is a natural desire and for most batsmen it is essential. The great South African batsman, Barry Richards, is the only batter I've ever seen who seemingly stood still until the ball was bowled. But video analysis reveals that he was also unweighting at this point.

Intending to go forward

The most important thing is to make any movement as efficient as possible. If you commit your weight to one foot or the other before the line and length is determined you will not have time to move that foot again. In my experience the overwhelming majority of top batsmen over the history of Test cricket have made a similar movement as the bowler prepares to deliver the ball. The movement indicates that the majority were preparing for the full ball until they were forced back. By preparing to go forward these players automatically adopt an ideal position of readiness. From this position they can easily continue to move forward or push back if forced to do so by the length.

This is not only the best position for most players to achieve at the point of delivery, but it is probably the only position from which they can easily move to the correct position for any length delivery. I believe this because the earliest indication you get from a bowler is that the ball is full, because it leaves the hand near the top of the bowling arc. If the release point is later the ball will be short of a full length. By being ready to go forward you are in the perfect position to respond to the full delivery. If the ball is short you have time to plant the front foot to push yourself back. This is not true of the reverse situation. Try it for yourself.

The one thing that is destined to undermine balance and the ability to assume the correct body position for each delivery is a commitment to one foot or the other before line and length are determined. Once the heel of the leading foot makes a definite ground strike you will not be able to use that foot again in any meaningful way during that delivery. It is essential to keep your weight predominantly on the balls of your feet during the decision-making phase for each shot. Once the decision is taken about where the feet need to go, then and only then can the leading heel be planted. The planting of one heel or the other is the trigger to deliver the bat.

Other aspects of balance

Body position and bat-swing are the other important aspects of balance. If the body is in the correct position for the intended shot then a good bat-swing path is assured. But if the body is out of position then the bat-swing will need to be manufactured. We have all been told that batting is a side-on activity. Unfortunately that phrase is often misunderstood and has led to many batting faults. While the stance is usually taken up side-on to the direction from which the ball will be delivered it is essential to place your body side-on to where you intend to hit the ball. By getting side-on to the intended line of the shot it will allow the bat-swing to be natural and, provided the follow-through goes along the intended path, the ball can be hit with power, control and precision.

The better players of each era have usually been the best at achieving the correct body position for the shot they intend to play. Sachin Tendulkar is the standout player of the current era because he has the best balance and gets his body in the best position for each delivery. Brian Lara would be the next best, Steve Waugh was very good, and Ricky Ponting is getting better all the time.

Timing — putting it altogether

Here and there, past and present, are relative not absolute and change
according to the coordinates selected.
EINSTEIN'S SPECIAL THEORY OF RELATIVITY

I've never heard whether Einstein played cricket — I don't think so. But his special theory of relativity has special meaning to cricketers, in fact to all sports people. To put it scientifically, Einstein discovered that the awareness of position and the motion of the body are relative to the requirements of the external demands. In a situation where the response is appropriate to those external demands, perception will slow down and there will be a feeling of timeliness.

So let's put it in layman's terms and relate it to cricket. When we watch a cricketer in action, or any athlete for that matter, we're actually watching 'timing'. Your position on the field (or in the grandstand) changes how the timing of that action or movement is perceived. For example, if you stand at cover-point you will have a different perception of the moving ball than someone standing at mid-off. It's different for everyone — from the slips fielder to the batter. So while the speed of the ball is the same, the perception will be unique for any given individual player. The harnessing of this perception into a good end result is timing.

In cricket, timing is a fascinating subject and one that hasn't received sufficient attention in the past. When Bradman once said that great batters were characterised by extra time to play the ball, he was highlighting the fact that they had come closest to perfecting their movement patterns and therefore maximising their response to the ball. The movement patterns, of course, are unweighting, coiling, using levers and balance. In addition, these batters had developed a large memorybank of experiences which they combined with this perfected movement to respond to the bowling. The same applies to the best bowlers who combine their memory bank of experiences with perfected movement to bowl consistently good balls.

At the beginning of this chapter I said that although we were examining the movements of unweighting, coiling, using levers and balance one by one for ease of explanation, in the end they have to be one total, fluid movement regime. This is where they all come together — in timing.

TIMING — BATTING AGAINST SPIN

One of the great joys of cricket is taking on a spin bowler like Abdul Qadir or Shane Warne. Against a spin bowler the batter has more time to weigh up the variables and make a decision about movement, so it makes sense to use this time rather than committing to a shot too early. Research indicates that the timing of a batter's swing from the top of the back-lift to the point of contact with the ball is pretty much the same regardless of whether you're facing fast bowling or slow bowling. So the timing of the movement is critical. Next time you see a batter having problems playing spin, watch it closely. It will probably be their timing. That's why, if you are young or out of form, a great training tool is to practise in the nets against spinners. It will help you get the timing of your movement right, and you'll be amazed how quickly your form returns.

So timing is the optimal sequence of unweighting, coiling and using levers in response to a demand. That demand might be, in the case of a bowler, to pitch the ball on a good length just outside the off stump. Or, in the case of a batter, it might be to drive that ball through the covers. But if the unweighting occurs slightly early, thereby setting up a chain reaction where your coiling and levers are premature, then your timing will be out and the shot will not be played (or the ball will not be bowled) at its maximum potential. Likewise, if you're not doing one of the movements correctly, for instance, exaggerated movements in your arms but small movements in your legs, you will create balance problems which, in turn, will effect your timing. That is why it's a whole movement regime, not separate movements; and that is why I say 'You can't teach it, each individual has to learn it.' But I have a lot more to say about teaching and learning in the section 'Creating the supportive learning environment' in Chapter 3.

DEFENCE

I purposely haven't talked about defence and there are good reasons for it. Let me explain. The purpose of batting is to score runs. Therefore the batter should play each ball with the intention of scoring runs if possible. The term often used is playing each ball on its merits with the intention of scoring runs. But sometimes the ball that is bowled forces the batter to defend. It might be a short ball at the body, a yorker or a cleverly flighted ball. However, there are two reasons why I see no need to talk about it. One, if your unweighting, coiling and levers are correct it is easy to turn your intention to attack into a defensive shot. Two, your brain tells you automatically when you're in danger and to defend. Take a look at these two photographs of Sachin Tendulkar. His 'set-up' for the shot, that is his unweighting, coiling and using levers, are the same for each. Sachin is always looking to score runs, but there are times when he is forced to defend.

For a bowler, timing is about two things:

- a smooth sequence of movements;

- optimising the release of the ball so it will have the desired affect.

To the spectator or coach good timing is most commonly viewed as a smooth, efficient run-up, a fluid and balanced action, and the resultant ball doing what was intended. It's the trademark of great bowlers such as Lillee, Hadlee, Sobers and Warne. Take the time to check for yourself next time you're at a game or watching cricket on television. You'll notice that any adverse variance during the bowler's movement sequence will cause an adverse result in overall timing, which in turn will cause an inconsistent end result. If this does occur the bowler (and/or coach) will attempt to diagnose which part of the movement sequence — that is, the unweighting, the coiling and the use of levers — didn't happen in a timely fashion and will try to solve the problem, hopefully with the next ball.

Richard Hadlee, Garfield Sobers and Shane Warne show perfect timing on delivery of the ball. Note the balance and the position of release, and the power that's been transmitted to the projectile (the ball) no matter whether it's fast, medium or slow.

> **BOWLING — TWO IMPORTANT POINTS**
>
> - If you are forced to cut short your coiling as a result of an inefficient run-up and/or jump, or you put significant pressure on the heel at back-foot landing, this will severely effect the body's ability to generate and transfer the forces that are critical to bowling.
>
> - If you unweight and coil incorrectly, this effects the distance over which your bowling arm rotates and, in turn, your ability to generate momentum.

Because the movements are so interdependent, the initial unweighting is very important. In batting, if you commit yourself on your first movement forward or back by making a significant heel strike, this will trigger the brain to release the hands into the shot, therefore committing you to the shot too early. What happens is this:

- You get yourself into a bad position from which you can't recover in time. (You only get one chance per ball to plant your foot!)

- You restrict your ability to track the ball.

- Your timing is lost because (a) you are there too early, almost groping for it, and (b) you are not tracking the ball as far as possible.

Try it and you'll see what I mean. The further away from your eyes and body you play the ball, the harder it is. You're there too soon and not connecting at the right stage of the bat-swing. Your timing will be out and the ball won't strike the centre of the bat — for example, instead of it flying through the covers, you might get a thick edge that flies through the gully. On the other hand if your initial movements leading to your levers are well timed, you'll be balanced and amazed at how long you can hold that position if you need to adjust your timing.

So the upshot of this is that you need to time the unweighting into the active neutral position ideally for each bowler. Researchers have set up mini-cameras that watch players' eye movements — it's been done in cricket, tennis and baseball as well as other sports. And they have shown that the better players wait a fraction of a second longer before committing themselves to an end position, which also allows them to track the ball better after release. It may be only fourteen thousandths (0.014) of a second longer, but it's the difference between perfect timing and average timing.

Timing — fast or slow bowlers

In batting, your timing will vary depending on the type of bowler. You will time your movements differently for facing Brett Lee to facing Shane Warne, or on a wicket that's hard and fast compared to one that's slow and turning. But research also tells us that the actual time taken to play the shot — from the top of back-lift to making contact with the ball — is similar for each type of bowler and consistent for each batter. So what we do is *hasten* our initial movement for fast bowlers and *delay* our initial movement for slow bowlers. And that makes sense because obviously you've got to be in position earlier to counter the blistering pace of Brett Lee bowling at 160 kilometres per hour than you do for Shane Warne bowling at 85 kilometres per hour.

How do the better batters like Adam Gilchrist and Matthew Hayden delay their movement? I mean it's pretty awesome facing bowlers like Brett Lee, Shoaib Akhtar, Curtly Ambrose and Michael Holding. I put it down to the fact that they have more skill, confidence and experience, so they are prepared to wait that little bit longer. Lesser skilled or untrained players, however, will want to get moving as quickly as possible. The problem with this is that once you commit to a hitting position you actually stop tracking the ball. So good players sight the ball longer because they have unweighted ideally and therefore can track the ball for longer.

Speed of movement

There's another point to make on timing too. Often, less confident players speed up their movements with fast bowlers and then retain that movement pattern with slow bowlers. This means the timing of their levers will be astray — and it's the use of levers that is a critical part for getting power, timing and placement correct.

This same problem occurs with top-class batters who are out of form. They're so anxious to make sure they're doing the right thing (to get moving) that they make the commitment too early and put themselves in a position they can't change. So you see them playing at the ball too far out in front of their body. It looks ungainly because they're anxious, nervous and lacking in confidence — simply put, they're out of form. I remember the form slump that I had in my career — I was doing the same thing. My arms were tense and I was playing the ball a long way from my body. It was the same for Allan Border, Mark Taylor and Steve Waugh.

But if you see the same batters when they're in full flight, or batters like Mark Waugh, Ricky Ponting and Sachin Tendulkar, everything looks free-flowing and fluent. They've made the right decision and they've come from the right position. Ricky Ponting went through a period where his form was indifferent. He was obviously anxious and you could see that he was committing himself onto the front foot much too early. This meant he was trying to play the ball from a fixed position, and if it deviated slightly he would be forced to release the bat early, resulting in his hands being a long way from his body at the point of impact. But good players in form get themselves into better positions because they come from the right unweighted position to begin with.

In addition, the top players take timing to another dimension. They actually adjust their levers to create perfect timing or change a shot. For instance, they might change their stride and instead of hitting the ball through mid-off, they hit it in front of square leg. They adjust their timing, their levers and their coiling to suit the conditions or what they're trying to achieve with that particular delivery. This way they can put pressure back on the bowler and start to break up the field. Sachin Tendulkar is very good at this. And in the latter stages of the 2003 World Cup, Ricky Ponting adjusted his levers to hit the ball long distances in the air.

Perfectly timed: Don Bradman, Ricky Ponting and Sachin Tendulkar. Note the way they are all perfectly balanced, the way the bat meets the ball at exactly the right time and the power with which the ball is being hit.

Now you understand Newton's Laws of Motion as they apply to natural human movement … and cricket. And how Einstein links them with timing. Understanding and perfecting these core principles, not technique, is what makes successful cricketers as you will further understand when you read chapter 3.

A TWENTY-POINT PLAN FOR BATTING AGAINST SPIN BOWLING

1   Have a plan.

2   Prioritise survival and scoring.

3   Practise both 1 and 2 at training.

4   Remember good spinners will always take wickets, but good batters make them pay a higher price.

5   Dictate to the bowler, don't let the bowler dictate to you.

6   Bat at your pace and rhythm, not theirs.

7   Use your feet to change the bowler's length.

8   Remember that there are two methods: cross-over or skip step. (The cross-over is smoother as the head stays still; you also cover more ground.) Stay on the balls of your feet.

9   Be positive with your foot movements.

10 Staying in your crease may not be the best solution.

11 Be prepared to attack spin bowlers from the front and back foot.

12 When going back to a ball spinning in from the off, maintain a body position that allows you to play on both sides of the wicket.

13 Bat in partnerships.

14 Rotate the strike.

15 On spinning wickets watch the ball more closely, but remember that the spinning ball has as many positive options as negative ones.

16 Look for balls that pitch wide of the stumps — they're scoring opportunities.

17 Force the bowler or captain to change the field.

18 If the ball spins a lot don't panic. In these situations the bowler can have just as many problems as you.

19 For a ball pitching on off-stump and turning in, consider an off-stump guard. And for the opposite, a leg-stump guard. This allows for a greater number of scoring options.

20 If tied down don't panic yourself into playing a risky shot. Look for opportunities to rotate the strike.

CHAPTER 2

How the Brain Works

*If we hit every shot as well as we did our best ones, there would be no
Inner Game of Golf. But because of mental interference, few of us perform to our true
potential for more than brief moments at a time. Learning to get out of
one's way is the purpose of the Inner Game.*

W. TIMOTHY GALLWEY, *THE INNER GAME OF GOLF*

Ever since I was a boy, I've been fascinated by the concept of success and how
people and groups achieve it. Over the years I've read many autobiographies
about leading people in their respective fields and tried to piece together the
critical points in their development. Why is it that some people learn and grasp
ways of doing things easily so they become super-proficient while others don't?
What allows Sachin Tendulkar and Ricky Ponting to be great compared to
other first-class cricketers who work hard, are very proficient, but obviously not
as good? By answering these questions we are able to open up a vast area of
opportunity for a huge number of people. It's an area that's been a great
resource in the development of my principles.

In order to understand how we learn and develop, it's helpful to have a basic
understanding of how the brain works. Understanding how the brain works
can answer a lot of those questions of why we react in certain ways. Reaction,
as we discuss in chapter 3, is the principal concept of batting, and also of fielding and wicket keeping, so it's a key element in cricket and many other sports.
Understanding how the brain operates, therefore, can help you take significant
strides in your learning. In fact, I believe strongly that, *the brain is a better cricketer
than you'll ever be.*

What an amazing part of our anatomy the brain is! More complex than any computer, the brain's great advantage over its mechanical counterpart is its ability to reason intuitively. The computer reasons logically, but the brain goes that extra step, and it's testament to the power of the brain that most advances in computer science try to emulate its functions.

The brain

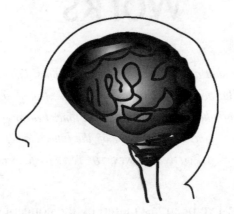

Even the most powerful supercomputers on the drawing board today pale into insignificance when compared to the brain's ability to work with metaphor and analogy, to see a logical sequence of events and then to go beyond, and take an incisive leap of insight. The insight might not seem to follow and yet the hunch will be correct.

CHARLES KREBS AND JENNY BROWN,

A REVOLUTIONARY WAY OF THINKING: FROM A NEAR FATAL

ACCIDENT TO A NEW SCIENCE OF HEALING

Charles Krebs is an astonishing guy, a former physiologist who suffered a life-threatening accident which rendered him a quadriplegic. But through his study of the brain and nervous system, from the points of view of both Western and Eastern medicine, not to mention his courage and tenacity, Charles fought his way back to walk again. He is now a kinesiologist based in Melbourne and has developed a ground-breaking approach to reintegrating brain function for those struggling to learn and perform. Although some find *A Revolutionary Way of Thinking* a fairly challenging book, when I first started reading it I just couldn't put it down. It's become my bible on how the brain and nervous system work.

The neuron

The basic unit that makes up the brain is the neuron (or nerve cell), and our brains have about a billion of them. There's said to be a trillion in the whole nervous system. Pretty mind-blowing stuff.

THERE ARE THREE TYPES OF NEURONS:

- SENSORY NEURONS, which deliver information from all parts of the body to the central nervous system, that is, the brain and spinal cord;

- INTERNEURONS, which connect the sensory neurons to other neurons and create networks that process sensory information; and

- MOTOR NEURONS, which send messages to the body's muscles to contract and relax.

All these neurons interconnect to integrate information, a key factor of brain function and what makes it so remarkable. For example, a neuron may receive information from an organ; it then passes that information onto other neurons in the chain and finally to its destination: muscles or other body parts that interact with the environment. But that's only half of it — for every neuron

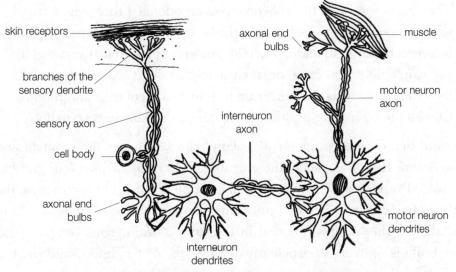

The brain — types of neurons and their structure. The billion or so sensory neurons, interneurons and motor neurons all interconnect, making it a mind-blowing piece of engineering.

there is a set of connectors called dendrites, axons and synapses that transfer information at extraordinary speed (hundreds of metres per second) through the nervous system. These neurotransmitters and receptors in each synapse open channels in the nerve membranes, permitting the rapid flux of small positive and negative charges that excite or inhibit action. So you can see why it's such a complex part of our body and why neuroscientists still have so much to discover about it. In fact it's this function of 'integration' in the brain that gives us the clue as to why 'integrating the parts into the whole' is the key factor in the core principles of movement (see chapter 1) and the learning environment (see chapter 3). Integration is the way the body works — the natural way.

The three tiers of the brain

The brain consists of three tiers (or layers); it has developed that way during the evolution of human beings. The oldest is the reptilian brain. It forms the central stem and controls our basic bodily operations such as heartbeat, breathing, temperature and intestinal functioning. Surrounding the reptilian brain is the limbic brain. In our early ancestors the limbic brain was actually the skin that covered the reptilian brain, but since those times it has enlarged and developed to provide many critical human functions. Charles Krebs describes it as well as anything I've read:

> The limbic brain is the subconscious emotional processing centre whose major role is to look out for the survival of self and the species. It directs the urge to mate, procreate, defend or submit. It says run if you can, fight if you can't, or stay where it's safe. It is also the part of the brain that elicits the nurturing response and controls and modulates all the basic built-in drives such eating, drinking and sexuality.

The third tier, the neocortex (or just plain 'cortex') encases the reptilian and limbic brains. It is often called 'the grey matter' because of its colour and has that 'folded' appearance you're probably familiar with. The cortex is the 'thinker'. Its functions include conscious thought and adding reason and rationality to the 'desires' created in the limbic brain. For example, your limbic brain is enjoying a particularly delicious meal of rich food and wants a third helping, but your cortex is saying, 'Enough is enough!', reasoning that to eat so much rich food is unhealthy.

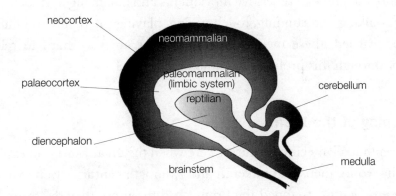

The three tiers of the brain: the reptilian brain, which controls the basic operation of the body; the limbic brain, which controls our basic urges and emotional needs; and the cortex, which does the thinking.

The cortex is divided into two halves: the left hemisphere and the right hemisphere. In turn, these are each divided into four sections called lobes: frontal, parietal, occipital and temporal. Each of the lobes performs different functions. The frontal lobes are where our thinking, reasoning and planning take place. They also control the eye muscles, the muscles for speech, and conscious direct movement. For example, if you decide to do a knee lift, it's your frontal lobes that direct the muscles to act. The parietal lobes process sensory information such as wetness, heat and pain and can memorise such things as touch. As the name suggests the occipital lobes are where the wonder of sight takes place; they can also store picture memories. Finally, we have the temporal lobes, which are the areas of the brain to do with speech, hearing, emotion and interpretation.

The cerebellum

'So, where's all the cricket action generated from?' you're asking. There is one further part of the brain called the cerebellum, which helps control our automatic movements and coordination — our subconscious movement. It is really important to cricket because it's one of the parts of the brain that we rely on for memorising shots, and for balance and equilibrium.

Cerebellum is Latin for 'little brain' and it's a kind of outcrop of the lower reptilian brain, just below and to the back of the cortex. The cerebellum 'learns', 'adjusts' and 'remembers' repetitive movements and balancing acts such as riding a bike, walking and running, touch-typing, playing the piano and hitting a ball. Once learned, these memorised movements are very hard to relearn. We'll work through this problem in detail in chapter 3.

The mapping of the brain

If the sixteenth to eighteenth centuries were when the great European explorers mapped the world, then the ninteenth and twentieth centuries were when the leading neuroscientists mapped the brain. And the more they discovered, the more complex and exciting they realised it was. They found that each section of the cortex controls, or is a sensory mechanism for, a certain part of the body — locating for example, the exact spots that control the movement of our fingers and thumbs, our legs and arms. They found the areas that gather sensory information, such as when you stub your toe. And they found that the control centres for body parts whose movements are the most complex (like the hands) or have the most sensation (like the tongue), occupy larger areas of the

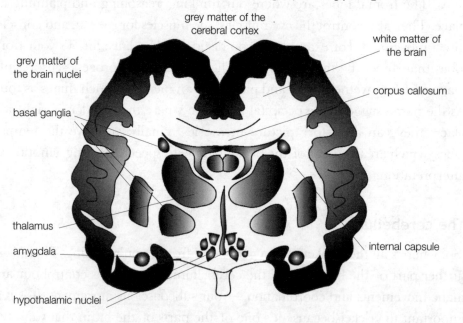

The cortex, also called 'the grey matter', is the part of the brain that controls our conscious thinking, reasoning, interpretation, speech, hearing and emotions. The cerebellum helps control our automatic motor functions and balance, for acts such as walking, riding a bike, playing the piano and hitting a ball.

brain — which makes sense, doesn't it? The more complex the movement, the larger the control centre. They found the sections where our free-thought and abstract thinking takes place; they found that the left hemisphere of the cortex controls logical and sequential functions, while the right hemisphere controls intuitive functions.

Often, of course, the decisions we make consist of both logical and intuitive thought. This is how Einstein developed his Theory of Relativity. He imagined himself travelling faster and faster until he reached the speed of light. As his speed increased he visualised himself becoming larger and larger. He then took this 'imaginary experiment' and proved it logically using mathematics.

The ninteenth- and twentieth-century neuroscientists also found that the brain is made up of two types of tissue: grey matter and white matter. The white matter is thought to consist of a hundred billion neuron-connectors that, like fibre-optic cables, carry the complex information instantly from one control base to another. Often decisions need various parts of the brain to interact — for example, the logical plus the intuitive, or speech plus movement. White matter is white because it consists of *myelin*, a kind of insulator for high speed communications that coats the neurons. Sometimes the myelin coating breaks down and the messages scatter away from their proper destination. This is what happens in multiple sclerosis, a debilitating disease whose symptoms include impaired vision, loss of balance and muscle coordination, slurred speech, bladder and bowel problems, difficulty walking, short-term memory loss, mood swings and, in severe cases, partial or complete paralysis. Having learnt a little bit about the brain you can now understand that if the messages are 'derailed', things are going to go wrong.

The grey matter is where the decisions are made, and consists of two parts: the outer section (the cortex) and a deep inner section of the limbic-reptilian brain, the brain nuclei. It consists mainly of interconnecting neurons (interneurons) cast like intricate 'nets' or 'webs' in the convoluted sheet covering the brain in the inner section. The cortex and the nucleus are the 'subconscious control stations' of the brain that process and integrate information, which is transmitted backwards and forwards via the white matter. And the two parts have different roles: the outer section for conscious response, thinking and decision-making, and the inner section for subconscious processing.

Functioning

You could liken the functioning of grey matter and white matter to the fielding team on a cricket ground. For instance, the captain looks at the scoreboard and decides something needs to be done to break a partnership. The captain discusses the situation with the vice-captain and then signals to a new bowler to come into the attack. The captain and bowler set the field and, meanwhile, the vice-captain has a few words of motivation to the surrounding fielders. Everyone's geared up for the breakthrough. Relating this to brain function, you could view the captain as the neuronal grey matter. The scoreboard, signals to players and conversations between players are the white matter carrying the information to organise the next stage of play. The vice-captain, the bowler and the fielders are the related grey matter areas of the brain that help provide the integrated decision to set up the right conditions for a successful outcome.

You could write a book or make a television series, and many people have, about the brain — there is so much fascinating and complex material to cover. But I want to look more closely at just one more aspect of the subconscious. Subconscious processing, as we discussed earlier, takes place deep in the limbic and reptilian sections of the brain, and one of the major areas is known as the *basal ganglia*. This is one of the largest groups of brain nuclei and a very complex area, but to keep it simple, it's where our learned subconscious movement sequences such as walking and running (and batting, bowling and throwing) are first created, and then stored for automatic use. What happens, for example, when a batter plays a shot? Most of the movement sequence is 'learned' by practice, and then largely subconscious when actually played. Really, the only conscious decision is whether to hit the ball; the decision whether to attack or defend is learned from practice and experience. The actual shot is made not by the conscious, but rather by a partnership between the basal ganglia and that other subconscious section of the brain, the cerebellum. Take the example of a back-foot defensive shot. This is often a subconscious reflexive action because it is fending the ball away and stopping it from hitting you. My software learnt this playing with my brother Ian in the backyard when we were kids. He was older and much bigger than I was and my brain had to learn quickly to look after me. What happens is, when the brain realises a short ball is heading for the body the 'control bases' deep in the limbic brain press an 'alarm button' and the subconscious automatically directs the body to take evasive action. I suppose the best example is the bumper when there is no time for conscious thought: the body just gets out of the way — fast.

So as my friend Charles Krebs says: 'What you do is decided by your cortex. How you do it is largely a subconscious process, one that is often affected by our subconscious emotional states.'

This is why learning the core movements of unweighting, coiling, balance and timing in the correct integrated sequence is so important. Because any repetitive, reactive movement becomes part of your subconscious — it's how the brain reacts to the pending challenge. And it's a lot of hard work trying to override the brain.

That's why I say, 'Let the brain do it for you — it is a better cricketer than you'll ever be.'

THE BRAIN AND THE ART OF BATTING

This text was compiled with the kind assistance of Dr Charles Krebs from his book, A Revolutionary Way of Thinking: From a Near Fatal Accident to a New Science of Healing.

1 When light enters the eyes, it is sent from the retinas to the visual thalamus (also called the lateral geniculate body or nucleus). The data from the retina is then split into three streams:

a. Via direct subconscious pathways to the amygdala, which assesses if the stimulus is potentially dangerous and, if so, activates withdrawal reflexes to move away from the object. This happens well before any of the semi-conscious or conscious processing has been completed in the cortex, because the amygdala makes only a coarse-grained image to assess potential threat and errs on the side of caution. That is, if it could potentially be dangerous, treat it as if it *is* dangerous!

b. Via the magnocellular pathways (called the m-pathways) to the exstriate cortex in the occipital lobes at the back of the brain, which processes the retinal information for the following components of vision in the following order of time. First, movement (whether moving or still); then location in three-dimensional space; then shape or form; and finally colour. This processing happens largely out of consciousness, and is completed before the final sharp, high resolution image is produced by the striate primary visual cortex.

c. Via the parvocellular pathways (p-pathways), which are smaller and hence slower than the m-pathways. The retinal information is processed through a number of layers of processing to create a sharp, high-resolution black and white image.

Through a trick of the brain, all of these separate processes happening in different places of the brain at different speeds are then suddenly unified into one seamless experience of a conscious sharp, high-resolution image of a specific object (say a ball) that is of a certain shape and colour and is moving in a particular direction from a specific place in three-dimensional space.

Since movement and direction of movement in three-dimensional space of a specific shape happen milliseconds before the actual object is recognised consciously, a long time in brain processing, the subconscious visual processing 'leads' the action about to be taken.

2   Muscle action, although initiated consciously, is run almost totally by the subconscious. For instance, when a batter is watching a ball approach, the consciousness sends out the command, 'Play the shot!' And the batter, from their conscious perspective waits until just the right time before moving to hit the ball.

As the ball approaches, the batter consciously initiates the command, 'Play the shot!' Using a computer analogy, this downloads an automatic pre-recorded generalised 'playing the shot' program stored in the putamen of the basal ganglia. (This is what practice is all about: creating these automatic programs.) This initiates the globus pallidus of the basal ganglia to run the 'playing the shot' program, organising all of the muscles involved in hitting the ball to become activated, and the movement begins.

At the same time, however, the cerebellum, a totally subconscious brain centre, is sent a copy of the 'intended action' to play the shot. Relying on much of the subconscious visual processing about ball movement and direction of movement in three-dimensional space, the cerebellum 'predicts' (by performing calculus) where the ball will be when it approaches the batter. Then, as the batter begins their movement, the cerebellum receives feedback from all of the muscle, tendon and joint proprioceptors: the subconscious sensors of the muscles, tendons and joints that give a read-out of muscles action, direction and speed of movement, and via tendon tension, the power of the swing.

So now the cerebellum 'knows' what shot the batter is actually playing, and it compares what is actually happening with the predicted position of the ball at the end of the movement. Since the cerebellum knows (a) what the intended action is (hit the ball), (b) the predicted position of the ball (which is constantly being updated), (c) what the 'actual' action is at that moment, and (d) the actual location of the batters feet, arms and bat, it can send out a corrective stream of motor signals directly to the motor cortex to modify the shot as it is taking place. This ensures that the *actual* action fulfils the *intended* action: hitting the ball.

Because so much of the control of motor action happens outside of their consciousness, the batter is then free to devote most of their mental resources to planning *where* they want to hit the ball and *how* they want to hit the ball. The 'where' and 'how' of this conscious intent continually modify the cerebellar 'intended' action. This results in the whole series of events above being repeated over and over as the ball approaches with the batter constantly modulating their movement, until, if the batter is successful, the bat makes contact with the ball.

Indeed, one of the differences between an experienced batter and a relative novice is that the experienced batter has had more successful experiences, and thus stored many more specific pre-recorded motor programs to better match the exact delivery at that moment. Thus there is less fine-tuning required by the cerebellum to make the intended action the actual action! And, of course, the experienced batter has also 'been there before' emotionally, and developed effective mechanisms to handle any stress more effectively than a less experienced batter. Since there are direct pathways from the subconscious emotional survival centres to the basal ganglia controlling the automatic movements of batting, this emotional input may subtly disrupt the precise timing needed to hit the ball. This is why when batters try to smash the ball out of the park, they often miss it altogether or hit it poorly.

But that's not all. Because the amygdala that runs the 'fight or flight' reaction actually fires first, before even the basal ganglia programs are fully activated. If the amygdala perceives the ball as a threat, it may fire an opposing motor program of 'withdrawal' rather than 'approach' which the consciousness requested. Since the amygdala represents survival programming, it will override the conscious desire, and the actual action will be more withdrawal than approach. Thus, some batters, perhaps those who have been hit and injured (pain activates amygdaloid memory), will actually have a very difficult time going onto the front foot when batting, often ruining their best efforts.

Finally, the movements of the bowler are processed rapidly by the subconscious extrastriate visual cortex involved with detecting movement, direction of movement in three-dimensional space, and the totally subconscious processing of the cerebellum that predicts the likely outcome of the bowler's movement. Thus the batter bases much of their subsequent conscious shot-making, and choice of how and where to hit the ball, on these predicted actions of the bowler. So, while the conscious intent of the batter constantly guides the action, a whole series of subconscious processes both about the shot and the bowler's likely delivery determine the outcome of the actual shot.

Now we can see why a batter needs a variety of experiences to develop the 'software' to be able to play well under all conditions.

How we learn

We never stop learning.
ANON

Just as it's important to know how the brain works, if we can understand how we learn we can open our minds up to more knowledge and opportunities. It might be a bowler working on their run-up to smooth out their action and create greater control; or it might be a coach who, by understanding more about how people learn, can offer greater help and guidance to their players. I can't define learning any better than Charles Krebs.

LEARNING is the ability to acquire knowledge or skills through experience or instruction. And it's the ability to modify our behaviour in response to a new experience based on our *memory* — what cognitive scientists refer to as 'learning transfer'.

MEMORY is the storage of knowledge and experiences, and the ability to use our memories to function well.

Without *memory*, *learning* is impossible.

Memory

Our memory bank is a very complex brain function so I'm not going to discuss it in detail. But scientific discovery over the last decade has shown that memory doesn't have its own specific section in the brain; instead, the process is widely distributed throughout. Like the other brain functions, memory is an integrated process and, generally speaking, it falls into two main types: conscious and subconscious. Although these two categories may occur in different parts of the brain, they operate together to process, store and retrieve memories.

Reward and punishment

A fascinating aspect of memory is that some experiences we choose to remember and some we totally forget. Some of our memories last forever, but some last less than a minute, so we find ourselves asking, 'Where did I put the car keys?' Researchers have shown that we only remember things that the brain associates with pleasure or pain (for example, reward or punishment, and success or mistakes); in other words, we only remember things that have had a positive or negative emotional effect on us. If an experience or event has no emotional impact then we forget about it.

Learning

What and why we remember has a very strong influence on learning — we tend to learn from those events for which we've received some reward or punishment. Think about it. When you do well at something and you feel good, you remember it. If you do it well a number of times it will pass to your long-term memory and you can say you've learned how to do it well. Also, when you make a mistake, such as burn your fingers on the barbecue, you remember (learn) not to do it again. In other words, you've learned that barbecues can hurt you unless you handle them properly.

Subconscious long-term memory

Our memory bank, our subconscious memory, directs our emotions and forces us to act in certain ways. For example, a subconscious long-term memory can override the conscious brain's desire to do something — especially something that the subconscious has learned is dangerous. I remember one of the guys at the Redbacks, the South Australian state team. He was a fine batter with good skills, a good run-scorer. But once the bowling got faster than 130 kilometres per hour, he would have problems. Instead of getting behind the ball he would become nervous and take evasive action. It really used to concern me because here was a guy with real talent, but when the ball got fast his brain said, 'Danger!' and his subconscious memory overruled his conscious desire to make runs and said, 'Okay, that's it, we're out of here!' So we worked hard on re-educating his subconscious memory so it could re-learn that the best method to deal with very fast balls is to play with correct technique and not to shy away from them — which often gets you in more trouble.

Learning and memory

So learning depends on memory. Without memory we would make the same mistakes time and time again, and our successes wouldn't be learned either, they'd be a one-offs, flukes. But I asked the question earlier, What makes one person better at their job, or more proficient at a sport, than someone else? What allows Sachin Tendulkar and Ricky Ponting to be great when other cricketers are simply good? The answer is, *they are better learners.*

Memory banks

Cognitive researchers have shown that high achievers gain more knowledge about what they're doing. This affects what things they notice, how they notice, and how they organise and interpret these things relative to their environment. So they build better memory banks, they reason better, and they solve problems better. You'd have to agree this pretty much explains the batting abilities of Sachin and Ricky and the bowling abilities of great bowlers like Shane Warne.

In chapter 3 we talk extensively about the importance of adding to your memory bank as many experiences as possible in as many different environments as possible, so that you can draw upon them to be able to deal with all eventualities in your game.

> Your learning environment is very important. It should be encouraging; it should give you a broad range of experiences such as success, fear and stress in as many different situations as possible; and it should be as natural (intuitive) as possible.

Complex environment — many experiences

Researchers have shown that animals brought up in their natural environment — that is, complex environments where they have lots of experiences — have more nerve-cell blood vessels and a greater supply of blood to the brain than animals brought up in captivity. Their larger memory bank of experiences gives them increased brain function and greater abilities. It's interesting that nearly all of the world's great cricketers in the first century of cricket learned to play the game naturally. And many of the best modern cricketers grew up learning the game in a rural or semi-rural environment, away from the coaching structures of the city. Kapil Dev, Adam Gilchrist, Matthew Hayden, Michael Holding, Glenn McGrath, Malcolm Marshall, Javed Miandad, Ricky

Ponting, Abdul Qadir, Andy Roberts, Michael Slater and Mark Taylor are just a few of the top modern cricketers who grew up in a natural learning environment.

Motivation

Provided the brain functions normally, the key to learning is motivation, and we can be motivated in several different ways, for example by relevance, emotional impact, interest, passion, love and fear. If our brain considers something to be irrelevant to our needs, such as learning maths at school when you want to be an actor, the brain is not going to be motivated to take in all that mathematical information. Lack of interest is also a demotivator to learning — just as acute interest is a strong motivator. Likewise, both passion or love for something, and fear of something, arc probably the strongest motivators of all. If you grow up being passionate about your cricket like my brothers, Ian and Trevor, and I did, you can't help but learn and become proficient.

Research has shown that learning requires a conscious effort, and conscious effort or intent is most successful when the person is enjoying what they are learning. Think about a few of the learning situations you've been in — when you've found the process easy and enjoyable and when you've found it difficult and a drag. The most successful learning experiences are when you're having a good time and are very motivated. This doesn't mean to say it's not hard work, but it's the enjoyment and the willingness to learn that are key factors. No one cares about how hard the work is when they're truly motivated.

Learning blocks

If a person's learning is not happening or difficult it is said to be 'blocked'. Learning blocks can have a number causes, but the two most common are:

- **PHYSICAL BLOCKS** — These can occur in three main ways: during foetal development of the brain if, for instance, it doesn't form properly; through micro-bleeding at childbirth, which can lead to the brain cells being starved of oxygen; and through severe head injuries at any time of life.

- **FUNCTIONAL BLOCKS** — These are the most common form of learning block and appear to be caused by stress. When the block is about something important it can cause problems with your confidence and self-esteem. This is why learning to handle stress so it works for you rather than against you is so important.

So despite the enormous complexities of how the brain operates, for most of us a positive attitude to learning and a good learning environment is all it takes to become proficient; you have to want to learn, you have to be passionate about what you want to learn. Problems like stress can be overcome provided you have an environment that encourages learning. The brain, through its integration of sensory information, directs the body's movements from the subconscious, pretty much automatically. That's why in developing your cricket skills the Chappellway we like to use complete, integrated movements and actions, steering away from single-action or part-movement drills. Understanding how the brain works and how we learn helps you gain a foundation of what governs the body's reflexes, emotional reactions and movement. This forms the basis of the next chapter, where we discuss good ways to learn and practise, and good ways to fix bad learning.

CHAPTER 3

The Learning Environment

It was fun and highly competitive, and we learnt to play in a number of very different conditions. Our parents too were very supportive. It was an unstructured and creative environment, the ideal way to learn the game.

The concept for this book started taking shape when I was coaching the Southern Redbacks. My daily work involved the minute detail of developing and implementing coaching and training strategies for both the high-performance South Australian state team and for South Australian cricket at all levels. And the thing that really amazed me was how much cricket had changed from when I played for the same team at the same ground thirty years earlier.

During its first one hundred years, cricket didn't change much at all. It was very unstructured and there was very much an intuitive approach to learning and playing the game. But since the Centenary Test Match between Australia and England in 1977, learning and playing cricket has become increasingly structured, with various sophisticated training techniques, performance-enhancing systems, computerised monitoring, fitness regimes and psychological testing. Australia pioneered this new technological approach, our team became the best in the world, everything seemed fantastic.

As I continued coaching I soon realised that the intuitiveness, one of the key learning elements of cricket's first century, had all but disappeared. When I would talk to the guys in the team about a certain batter or bowler, or a series against another country from just a few years before, they would stare at me blankly. They had *played* a lot of cricket, but they hadn't *watched* a lot of cricket. My brothers, Ian and Trevor, and I grew up learning and understanding the game by a kind of osmosis. We played a lot of cricket in the backyard, we talked a lot about cricket and, importantly, we watched a lot of cricket. We absorbed it. There was no television and there were no television commentators. You actually had to go to a cricket match for four or five days and watch. If you missed something there was no replay. I know now that I learnt so much and I didn't even know I was learning. There was information going into my software that I wasn't even aware of — the nuances, the ebb and flow of the game. It was a critical part of my learning process.

Now I'm not suggesting for a minute that we go back to the old days. I believe we should grab with both hands anything and everything we can to improve our game. But we shouldn't forget that the unstructured, intuitive environment produced many great cricketers who we can learn from. It was an excellent learning environment.

TWENTY-FOUR TOP CRICKETERS FROM THE FIRST CENTURY OF CRICKET WHO LEARNED THE GAME IN AN UNSTRUCTURED, INTUITIVE ENVIRONMENT

BATTERS		BOWLERS	
Don Bradman	Bill Ponsford	Bishen Bedi	Bill O'Reilly
Greg Chappell	Viv Richards	Lance Gibbs	Erapalli Prasanna
Ian Chappell	Garfield Sobers	Wes Hall	John Snow
Sunil Gavaskar	Victor Trumper	Michael Holding	Jeff Thomson
Len Hutton	Clyde Walcott	Harold Larwood	Fred Truman
Graeme Pollock	Everton Weekes	Dennis Lillee	Derek Underwood

The importance of childhood learning

We were very lucky that we grew up in a sporting family. Our father was a keen sportsman; he represented South Australia at baseball and he'd been in the State cricket squad. But when he was twenty World War II broke out and his best sporting years were lost to the war. I didn't ever speak to him about it, but

I have realised since that he probably became frustrated at not achieving his goals in sport, especially cricket. So he put that energy back into his kids: 'I'll make sure the boys get the opportunity I never had.'

Our grandfather, our mother's father, was Vic Richardson, who played test cricket for Australia. Obviously he was a keen sportsman too, so our mother had grown up in a full-on sporting environment; and for as long as I could remember the conversation around the dinner table, the breakfast table, and most other times was generally about sport. Dad always encouraged us. Like him, we played cricket all summer and baseball all winter. Cricket and baseball are very compatible sports because they have so many similarities. But they are also different enough that by the end of the cricket season you'd be looking forward to a game of baseball; and by the end of the baseball season you couldn't wait for the cricket season to begin again. So we always had a bat and ball in our hands: throwing, catching, hitting — hand–eye coordination sports. And if there wasn't anyone to play with, I'd hit a tennis ball or cricket ball up against the back wall, or throw a golf ball against the base of the tank stand and it would fly back at different angles — a great way to sharpen your reflexes.

All the things we did just messing about were, in fact, training for skills that would be very important later on.

We always had a bat in our hands

Our father also encouraged us by having us coached by a family friend who'd been a very good country cricketer. His name was Lynn Fuller and he'd been a farmer so he was never able to play with the major teams in the city. After Lynn retired from the land he lived just around the corner from us in North

Glenelg, Adelaide, and set up a couple of practice wickets in his backyard. Most of the boys from the neighbourhood used to go there on Sunday mornings and Lynn would give us some coaching. It was pretty basic stuff: forward defence, back defence, the cover drive. The lessons used to last about half an hour each.

Fun at home

But what I remember more than anything else was that, after we'd finished with Lynn, we would go into the other net and Dad would throw balls to us. He would throw all kinds of balls — long hops, half volleys, wide ones, full tosses — with the idea that we would try to hit them to score runs. Dad's theory was this: a batter is there to score runs, but in order to do that you need a good defence and sound technique. So Lynn taught us the fundamentals and Dad taught us how to bat. Later, Dad built us a practice wicket in our own backyard and when we weren't at Lynn's place we would be home, with Dad throwing balls at us there.

Lynn wouldn't take us in his coaching sessions until we were five years old. When I was four I used to go down and watch my brother, Ian, who's five years older than me, and the big guys. It was a very long wait, waiting to turn five. But worse was to come. I remember, three weeks before my fifth birthday, I was pushed off a fence in the backyard and landed on my left arm. I was in agony for a couple of days until mum finally took me to the doctor. It turned out I had a greenstick fracture and ended up with my arm in plaster from the hand to the elbow. So my debut at Lynn's coaching school had to be put on hold. I've never been so disappointed in all my life. Finally, though, my chance came and for the following five years I went to Lynn's and Dad's coaching clinic every Sunday morning.

It seemed that anyone who wanted to could go to Lynn's place on Sunday mornings. There was Ian and me (and later on Trevor, who's nearly five years younger than me); Lynn had two boys of his own; there were various other locals and some kids who travelled from other suburbs. I remember Neil Dansie, who later played for South Australia, used to come on the tram with a couple of his friends. I don't know whether Dad ever paid for the coaching: I don't think so. I think it was a labour of love for Lynn. He just loved his cricket and wanted to pass on the basics of the game to young kids.

A range of experiences

Another critical part of our development was that every waking hour possible we played cricket — in the backyard, in the park and down at the beach. If there were only two or three of us we would play in the backyard. If there were more than that, we would go to the park around the corner. There was also another park about a mile away from home, and during the holidays there would always be twenty kids down there. So, if we wanted a real contest, we'd get the kids from our little neighbourhood — usually about eight of us — and head over to that park. We'd form teams and play five test matches in a day! We never took drinks or anything to eat for lunch — there was a tap in the corner of the park to get a drink if we wanted something. And we'd just play all day, stagger home in the late afternoon and gulp something down then.

If it was summertime and really hot, we'd generally go to the local park in the morning and, as it got hotter, head down to the beach in the afternoon, where we'd play on the sand. At the beach we'd use a tennis ball. We'd shave the fur off half the ball so it would swing and loop. We'd start off on the soft sand and rough it up to make a bumpy pitch so the ball would swing and bounce all over the place. We'd have fielders all around the bat and you had to learn how to handle a ball that swung in the air and bounced every which way. Then we'd go down to the wet sand on the edge of the water where you could bowl bouncers or make the ball skim — even the little kids could dig the ball in and bowl a bumper. It was creative play and a lot of fun, and very competitive. No one wanted to get out, but if you did, you got another hit when your turn came around in the next half-hour or so, so it was no big deal.

At primary school we would all get there by 8.00 a.m., about an hour early, and there would be about thirty or forty kids with only one bat and ball, all playing cricket. It was 'gets out goes in', meaning if you bowled or caught someone you got to be the batter. So you'd be knocking kids over to take catches or to get the ball and have a bowl. Obviously the better ones got more opportunities than the weaker ones, so it was survival of the fittest. It certainly wasn't egalitarian.

Imagination

The other cricket activity that consumed us was playing make-believe test matches in the backyard. Because of the age differences between my brothers and me, we were 'only children' in many respects for a large part of our early years. By the time I was born Ian was at primary school, so I had Mum to myself all through the day. Just after Trevor was born I started at primary school, and by then Ian had gone to high school. So it was really only when I was about nine that Ian recognised that I was alive, let alone that I might actually be able to participate in something he was doing. He and his mates would come home from school and I was always wanting to be involved, but they'd tell me I was too small and to shove off. But then, at some stage, he must have been short of a playing partner, looked around and realised I was getting a bit bigger and maybe I could play.

So we started playing our test matches in the backyard. They were always Australia vs England — they were the big test matches of the time. Being the older brother, Ian was always Australia, leaving me to be England. I remember it was a real conflict for me because I didn't want to be beaten by my older brother, but then I didn't have my heart in winning for England. Anyway I was stuck with it until Ian moved out of backyard cricket and Trevor moved in. Then I became Australia and he was England.

We would pick our teams and assume the identities of the great players of the day. Ian would be McDonald, Burke, Harvey, O'Neil, Burge, Benaud, Davidson and Lindwall, etc., and I would be Cowdrey, Edrich, Graveney, May, Statham, Truman, Locke and Laker, and so on. We simulated the atmosphere of a real test match every way we could so they were pretty intense games. Of course, we always used a hard ball — Dad encouraged us to do that so we'd get the feel of it. And when you went out, you had to go into the laundry and come back as the next batsman — you actually had to walk off the ground. I can even remember changing the pads, taking them off and putting them back on, and then walking out as the next batter; and if he was a left-hander you'd have to bat left-handed. Left-handers didn't make as many runs in our test matches! This became a real problem later on when Ian went to play cricket in England when he was eighteen. I became Australia and Trevor, who was nine by this stage, became England. One of my heroes was Neil Harvey, who was left-handed, so it really made me work hard. Being one of my heroes, Harvey had to make a lot of runs.

So this is how my cricketing brain was engaged. We were living these moments — they were real test matches — and it was a very important stage in my development as a cricketer.

The Chappell backyard practice wicket in Glenelg, Adelaide, home to many a fiery test match.

Backyard cricket matches

Perhaps in response to our cricket fever or the fact that we just about denuded the backyard every summer, Dad built us a turf practice wicket. It was made of regular turf, a black clay soil that bound really hard so that the ball had quite a bit of bounce. The soil came from the North Glenelg reserve where Lynn Fuller happened to be the curator. It was Athelstone soil, the same soil used for all the other turf wickets around Adelaide. The turf section was about 10 metres long and slightly raised from the surrounding earth so it had a ridge at the edges. Dad had built it wide enough so that we could just squeeze in three batting spots with the edges of each wicket overlapping. Luckily, our house block was about 24 metres wide so the pitch was aligned across the yard, which gave us a two or three-step bowling run-up.

On the off-side of our pitch was the house, which had quite a few windows. Windows and cricket, of course, don't mix. So Dad went to the rubbish dump and found some old wire mesh gates that he put up to protect them. On the leg side of the wicket there were a number of fruit trees — peaches, almonds, lemons, mandarins — which had trouble bearing fruit because we were continually knocking it off with the hard ball. So Dad built wire cages around them and they became fielders in our practice sessions and test matches. If you hit the wire on the full you were out. If you broke a window you were definitely out. Dad even built extensions on the side fences because the balls were going over and breaking the neighbours' windows. In the end our backyard was like Stalag 17!

Fielding and scoring was all worked out. If you nicked the ball and it hit the fence behind the wickets you were out. That was the slip cordon and the uprights designated the range of the keeper and each slips fielder. Anything wide of the designated positions was four runs. On the leg side we had a paling fence. Anything that hit the fence between the top and the bottom horizontal beams was out; and anything above or below the beams was not. With the addition of the fruit trees the leg side was well inhabited with fielders. But there was a gap between forward square leg and backward square leg, between the citrus and almonds, so the only place I could really hit the ball on the leg side with safety was just behind the square. That's how I learnt to pick the ball up off my hip. I had to get runs and not get out because if it hit the trees on the full I was dead.

THE FIRST LINE OF DEFENCE

You perhaps wouldn't think it, but playing backyard cricket with a hard ball and without any protective gear was a good way to learn about defence. I soon learnt, playing with my older brother Ian, that the first line of defence is the bat. If you hit the ball it can't hurt you. I learnt that important lesson about batting while messing about in the backyard.

As I mentioned, our pitch had a bit of a ridge on it. If Ian needed to get a wicket or wanted one to bounce around my head to soften me up, he was accurate enough to hit the ridge and the ball would come flying through. We had no helmets, no gloves, no box and often no pads, so we knew what it was like to be hit with the hard ball; and we were hit quite a few times. These days cricket administrators are very proud of their initiatives of independent umpires and referees, but we had our own referee all those years ago. If I found that things were going badly for me, and I made enough noise about it, Mum would always come out and see what was going on. I remember one day when Ian said that I was caught behind. We were arguing and fighting — the arguments and the fights were legendary — and Mum finally came out and said, 'What's going on, Ian, what's happened?' Ian replied, 'The little *so and so's* out and he won't go.' And then she asked me and I said, 'I didn't hit it, I'm not out.' So she said, 'Look Ian, he's younger and smaller, give him another hit.'

This happened more than a few times. It was another weapon in my defence against my older and stronger brother.

But for every time Mum the umpire ruled in my favour, I could expect pay-back in the form of a barrage of bumpers. Ian would push off a bit harder from the fence and aim at the ridge, and the balls would come flying around my ears. One day he hit me on the fingers. I'll never forget it. Boys weren't meant to cry in those days, but on this occasion I was down and out. I was lying on the pitch blinking back the tears and suddenly I was aware of this shadow hovering over me. Normally, Ian stood about 10 metres away and glared at me until I got up, but on this occasion he'd come right up the pitch. I thought, 'at last, a bit of compassion from the older brother'. So I looked up, tears in my eyes, and he said, 'I wouldn't worry about the fingers if I was you, it's your head next.' It was pretty willing stuff in the backyard; they were serious games.

So that was what we did as kids. Every spare moment was spent playing cricket and when we weren't playing it, we were watching it, listening to it on the radio, or talking about it.

Creating the supportive learning environment

Don't try to teach cricket. It's too difficult to teach.
Create an environment where cricketers can
learn *how to play the game.*

I tell this story with apologies to the sports mistress at a Sydney girls' school, but it illustrates a very important point. One of my friends had a daughter there and he called me and said, 'The girls are playing cricket and every week they're getting thumped because they just can't play. Could you come and help?' I went out to the school and watched how they were training. The sports mistress was a cricketer and she was *teaching* them how to play. Things like: 'Step to the ball, bend your front knee and the left elbow up'. But the kids weren't succeeding at all. They were tense and frustrated, and they weren't enjoying it because they simply couldn't hit the ball. So I suggested that I work with one group on their batting while the teacher took another group off for fielding practice.

Learning to enjoy cricket

The first thing I said was, 'Look, we're just going to have a bit of fun today. I want you to start off by forgetting everything you've ever been told about cricket.' My idea was that each girl would have a turn with the bat — just a few minutes — while the others who were waiting around could retrieve the balls. So the first one came up and I said, 'I just want you to watch the ball, move towards it and hit it. I'm going to throw them quite full for a start and then a little bit shorter each time until you're forced back by the length of the ball. I don't care whether you hit the ball in the air or along the ground. It doesn't matter where it goes. I just want you to hit it.' Within minutes they were all laughing and shouting: 'Oh look, it's gone over Sophie's head! Hey, it's gone for four!' It was almost the first time most of them had hit a ball. And it was the first time they'd had fun playing cricket. Suddenly they were having a bit of success — all within two hours.

The next week I went back again. This time the girls who were waiting around for their turn were not only fielders, they were also targets. Yes, targets! And I'd say, 'Hit one at Jane.' And I'd throw it so she could hit it at Jane. And with the next one I'd say, 'Hit it at Emma.' And I'd throw it so she could hit it at Emma. Again, it didn't matter where it went — the aim was to hit it. They were often unsure of themselves and would ask me, 'How do I hit it?' And I'd say, 'You'll work it out.' The first few they usually hit in the air, but it was amazing how quickly they adjusted and, by the end of the session, everyone was hitting the ball along the ground. I hadn't *told* them to hit it along the ground, and I hadn't *told* them how to hit it.

They were soon pulling and cutting the short balls, and hitting cover drives and straight drives when the balls were pitched up. They were even playing defensive shots. Now, I hadn't even mentioned that. But when I threw one a bit straighter and faster, they'd defend. It wasn't always the neatest shot in the world, but they stopped it — which is what defence is all about.

Natural movement

The transformation was amazing. I didn't *teach* them anything about cricket, I simply got them to watch the ball and move. Their brains organised the rest. And the interesting thing was that the first parts of their bodies that moved were their hips. As soon as I'd say, 'Hit one at Lucy,' their hips would start to rotate. Because that's what the body naturally does. When I see the ball leave the bowler's hand and decide to play a cover drive, the first movement is to shift my weight onto one foot to get the hips moving so I can move my body. This is the problem when coaches concentrate on things like bending elbows and positioning the feet. You feel stiff and ungainly. But if I said to you, 'Okay, hit it in that direction,' the first thing the brain does is shift the weight onto one leg to organise the movement. The whole body has to revolve and, as we've seen in chapter 1 that's what coiling is all about. When the body coils it stores energy. Then when you transfer the weight the body uncoils and you deliver the stored energy (power) to the ball.

In two sessions these girls had learned to play and enjoy cricket. I hadn't taught them. I'd simply created the right environment for them to learn.

Target practice

'Target practice' has been a really important cog in the development of my theories on the creative and unstructured learning environment and website, www.chappellway.com. It all began towards the end of my international career when my children were still young. Because I was away playing cricket so often my eldest son, Stephen, who was about nine at the time, would watch the test matches on television, and rather than emulate his dad he taught himself to bowl like Dennis Lillee. Stephen would watch Dennis bowl, grab a cricket coaching book to work out the bowling grip, then practise for hours out on the tennis court. He'd bowl at a target on the fence. We were living in Brisbane in those days and our house had a tennis court; and when I'd come home from a test match or series he would take me out onto the court to show me how he'd taught himself to bowl outswingers — just like Dennis Lillee.

Creative play

At about the age of six my youngest son, Jonathan, decided he wanted to play cricket. I'd retired from cricket by then and would come home from work pretty tired and Jonathan would say, 'Hey dad, come out and bowl to me. Come on!' I wouldn't be all that enthusiastic after a day at the office, but he'd get me out there and, as much for my own benefit as anything, I'd try to make it fun. He only had a small bat, a cut-down version of one of Stephen's old bats, and I would throw balls to him and give him targets to hit. I'd say, 'Hit the ball at that part of the fence. Hit the ball at the net post. Hit that target over there.' And I'd throw the ball so it gave him a fair chance of hitting the targets. We had a scoring system. He got four if he hit one target, two if he hit another, six if he hit something more difficult. The idea was that as soon as he got to 100 we could go inside. So I'd throw balls where he could hit a lot of fours and sixes and get to 100 really quickly. It goes to show just how sneaky parents can be. But we'd had fun — he was happy and I was happy — and he'd learnt how to hit the ball to score runs.

With bowling, Jonathan and I did much the same thing. But this wasn't my invention, it was Stephen's. I said, 'You'd better learn to bowl. I'm not going to *teach* you to bowl, you have to *learn*.' So we set up targets on the ground so he would learn to bowl a good length, and on the fence so he would learn direction. 'See if you can land the ball on that dark green patch there? That's the area for you to aim at. And see if you can hit the fence there. They're your targets.' So he'd run up and bowl. I didn't tell him *how* to do it; he simply *did* it. Like Stephen, Jonathan had seen a lot of bowling on television so he knew what it looked like — and kids are great mimics. I'd get him to aim for the targets to see how many times he could hit them out of ten. So, as with batting, he taught himself to bowl. I was simply the scorer, the umpire, and his support crew.

After a couple years I noticed that Jonathan had good hand–eye coordination, so when he was about eight I took him down to the Wilston Junior Cricket Club. Most states had cricket clubs with junior and senior sections, but Brisbane in those days had separate clubs for juniors. He turned up for the Under 10s and I was just staggered at the power of his shots and the way he bowled so straight. I remember watching him in a match one day on a ground that had a considerable downwards slope from the leg side to the off side. The kids were allowed to face 24 balls or make 20 runs (whichever came first), and bowl two overs each. Jonathan had to retire after five balls in the first over — he'd made his 20 runs. The most impressive aspect of his batting was the power. He hit a couple of pull shots for four up the hill — they didn't just trickle over the boundary, they were powerful shots.

You can guess the point I'm going to make, can't you. The environment that Jonathan learnt in was creative play with targets. I didn't teach him to bat and I didn't teach him to bowl. He learnt them himself. I didn't show him how to play defensive shots. But interestingly enough, when the ball was too difficult to play an attacking shot he would just stop it. And his technique was quite good. The brain organised it for him. His whole focus was looking for the ball to score runs and he tended to move forward unless he was forced back. He had developed a very natural style, which was logical when you think about it, because he had no real instruction at all. He had learnt in a totally free environment that had allowed for mistakes, and his creative instincts took over.

So target practice was a real lesson for me. My sons, one who's a pilot and the other who chose baseball as his sport, taught me that the less structured the learning environment the freer you are to develop your own style, whether it is batting or bowling … or flying an aircraft.

COURT CRICKET

You can play this game on any court: a tennis court, a basketball court, a volleyball court, a squash court, or even a *courtyard* — any restricted area. It's a fun game that helps you develop your own natural style as a batter, bowler and fielder. For batters it's a great way to learn how to score runs, for bowlers it's equally as good for learning to bowl line and length, and for fielders it really sharpens your reflexes because of the confined space of the court.

You will need:
- Two teams (preferably five per team, although you can play with fewer).
- Wickets about 10–12 metres apart.
- Four targets: one each side of the wicket, about 5 metres square of the batting crease (approx. short square leg and short point); and one each side, about 8 metres square of the bowling crease (approximately wide mid-on and wide mid-off).
- Set a value on your targets to suit your circumstances. Other runs can be scored by running between wickets.
- Any old bat.
- A tennis ball or any other ball appropriate for the court.

You can make your wickets and targets out of anything: pieces of cardboard or plywood, witches hats, sports bags, you can even draw them with chalk. But don't wreck the walls!

How to play:
- A game comprises one innings per team.
- An innings comprises five or ten 6-ball overs.
- Each batter faces a maximum of 6 or 12 balls (depending the length of the game).

- Batters score by hitting the targets or running between the wickets.
- Batters can be out bowled, caught or run-out only. Run-outs must be direct hits.
- Each player on the bowling team bowls one or two 6-ball overs (depending on the length of the game).

Have fun and be creative! Change the rules to suit yourself!

20-20-20-20 CRICKET — AN ALTERNATIVE COMPETITION FORMAT

Here's an alternative competition format, this time developed with the assistance of members of my website. A good thing about this format is that it gives both teams two innings each, but in less time than a standard one-day game. Of course, you can adapt the format for your own needs and timeframe.

BASIC RULES:

The game consists of eighty 6-ball overs — each team has two innings of 20 overs, each taken alternately. That is, Team A bats for 20 overs, bowls for 20 overs, bats for another 20 overs, then bowls for the final 20 overs, while Team B bowls first and bats last.

Each team bats for the full 2 x 20–over innings.

Bowlers can bowl a maximum of 6 overs over the entire game; however, two may bowl a maximum of 8 overs.

Batters retire once they have scored 30 runs. If all the batters have retired or been dismissed prior to the 20 overs being bowled, the batter with the lowest score bats again, and so on up the scorecard until the team has played out its 20 overs.

A team's score is determined by dividing the total score by the wickets lost. Retired batters do not count as wickets lost. The winning team is the one that scores the most runs per wicket.

Team points are allocated as follows:
- 6   points for a win
- 3   points for a tie
- 3   points for a draw

Team bonus points are allocated for:
- 0.01 points for each 10 runs scored
- 1   point for each 40 runs without losing a wicket
- 0.02 points for each wicket taken
- 1   point for every wicket bowled
- 1   point for every catch taken by the wicket-keeper, slips or gully fielders
- 1   point for a fielder effecting a direct-hit run-out
- 1   point for a wicket-keeper allowing less than 5 byes in an innings

All the other rules of cricket apply. And remember, adapt these ideas to suit your own needs.

The importance of learning and playing in different conditions

I've touched on this before, but I want to stress the importance of learning and practising under different conditions by giving it its own brief section. As I've mentioned, when my brothers and I were growing up we played in the backyard, at the park and on the beach. At each place the ball behaved and bounced differently. It was different for the bowler, different for the batter and different for the fielder.

Turf

On our turf wicket in the backyard, the ball had a fair bit of bounce and carry. But the bounce was even and the ball didn't turn much. Both as batters and bowlers we had to learn how to deal with it. We had to solve the problem of how a bowler gets wickets and a batter makes runs on a true and even pitch.

Grass

At the park the grass was always long, so the ball tended to stop a little bit and deviate — what we call 'seam' off the pitch. Sometimes we'd take the motor mower and mow a strip in the middle of the oval. When we'd finished we'd heave the mower to one side — we'd never bother taking it home — and start playing. These wickets were really green and juicy and the ball skidded off; it came onto you really quickly. Again in this environment we learnt different skills. We learnt how to score runs on a fast pitch and we learnt to take wickets.

Sand

At the beach, the tennis ball hitting the sand would behave differently again. It would come off very slowly with lots of bounce, so we learnt to play cross bat shots — cut shots and hook shots.

These skills were great later on when I had to succeed on wickets as diverse as the fast pitches in Perth, the soft wickets of England and the slow and dusty wickets of Pakistan and Sri Lanka. Being able to deal with all sorts of conditions helps you to become more consistent; and we all know that the best cricketers are consistent. They make runs, get wickets and field well under all conditions. Think about the good cricketers you know. Why are they good? They do well in all conditions.

BOWLING MACHINES — USE THEM WISELY

The reasons I encourage cricketers to learn, play and practise under many different conditions are the same reasons I discourage the current use of bowling machines. Bowling machines don't display the whole bowling movement. Repetitive work with a bowling machine trains timing patterns that are inconsistent with batting against a real-life bowler in a match situation. In other words the way a bowling machine works contradicts the central theory of the core principles of movement in chapter 1.

Let me explain. How, for example, can you unweight with the correct timing without the cues from a bowler's run-up and delivery action? A bowling machine only trains part of the batting action. Some will argue for using the machine to correct specific problems, but as they only train part of the whole we create the problem of transferring that part back into the whole movement pattern required in match situations. Use them to stimulate specific situations and they *may* have short-term benefit. Use them almost exclusively and they can compromise learning.

(We discuss this in a lot more detail under the heading 'Training for batting' on page 107.)

Learning to play under pressure

Contrary to popular thought, stress can be a good thing. Stress occurs when you raise the benchmark. If you are going to raise your cricketing benchmark by trying to improve and play to your full potential, you will encounter stress. The problem many cricketers and many other people have is that they don't learn about stress as they go along.

The following scenario is typical of how most young kids learn to play cricket. We have a young girl or boy who is ten years old and wants to play cricket. So Dad takes the child down to the local cricket club to play in the Under 11s. Practice is on Wednesdays and matches are on Saturday mornings. At practice the young cricketer gets ten minutes of batting in the nets, ten minutes of bowling, and ten minutes of fielding practice. Because they are new to the game, their skills have quite a way to go. However, they are selected for the team, Mum takes them to the sports store to buy some whites, and they turn up on Saturday morning excited and ready to play the game. So the kid sits there padded up ready to go in.

Structured learning

Because of the large number of activities kids do these days, and because play-ing on the street or in the local park can be dangerous, the extent of the kid's cricket-playing time is practice on Wednesdays and the match on Saturdays. If they go out after a couple of balls their cricket-playing time is hugely curtailed. This puts them under a lot of stress for which they've had no training. As they sit there waiting to go into bat, they feel pretty stressed. When they're out in the middle batting, it's worse. It's the same with bowling because they only get two or three overs, so the pressure is on to get a wicket virtually every ball they bowl. I believe this situation, which most young cricketers (as well as many senior cricketers) have to go through, is too difficult and too stressful, because most of them haven't learnt how to deal with the competitive pressure that occurs in match situations. I have a saying that sums it up: 'We send them off to cricket kindergarten on Wednesdays and cricket university on Saturdays.' The gap is too large.

Unstructured learning

When Ian, Trevor and I were growing up playing cricket in the backyard, at the park and on the beach, we were dealing with stress all the time. Because our games were very competitive we were desperately striving to get wickets or stay in to make runs and win the game. In hindsight, I can now understand that what we were doing was putting ourselves under continual stress. If you wanted to bat for any length of time you had to learn how to survive and devise ways of scoring runs. If you wanted to bat sooner rather than later, you had to learn how to get wickets so your turn to bat would come around again. So, without really knowing it at the time, we were continually stressing our nervous system. For example, down at the beach, the fielders would be all around the bat, hovering like vultures, and you had to find ways to survive and force them back. Then, down at the water's edge, we'd often throw and hurl the ball down rather than bowl it, anything to make sure the balls were fast and skimming through. We'd be as fast as Wes Hall, as wily as Alan Davidson, as strong as Keith Miller or as quick as Ray Lindwall. It was fantastic. We were continually under pressure, but we also had plenty of opportunities and plenty of fun. A kid who wasn't much of a spin bowler at the park would be getting heaps of turn and bounce at the beach. And the batter who had trouble at the beach would more than likely be successful in the backyard. So when it came to match day as it did when we grew older, it was just another competitive game. We'd already batted twenty or thirty times and bowled at least 50 or 60 overs during the week.

Practice time

So, if you learn how to deal with it properly, stress can be a good thing that can really drive your development as a cricketer. And although today's structured learning environment has some advantages, one of its by-products is the enormous amount of negative stress it puts on our kids. We can solve this problem by doing two things. The first is to encourage kids to learn the game with their family and friends in a free and creative environment, as well as in the structured environment of the cricket club or school. The second is to decrease the emphasis on net-practice and use a much greater proportion of practice time for match simulation. This way our kids would be continually learning to deal with the positive stress of competition in a real-life situation. This is covered in more detail on pages 96–99.

WHAT IS PRESSURE (OR STRESS)?

Pressure (or stress) is your emotional response to a specific situation. It usually manifests itself as a tight or sick feeling in the stomach. The better prepared you are for that situation, or the more experience you have had in similar situations, the better able you are to handle the emotions created by that situation. Batting in the nets, for example, is not as stressful for most people as batting in a match, with all the possible negative outcomes such as getting out, looking foolish or getting hurt.

A little bit of stress can be a good thing, as it will help to focus your mind on the task ahead. Too much stress can overwhelm you. It can trigger subconscious reactions that override the brain functions that are necessary for you to focus on batting or bowling.

The thought processes that are likely to cause you to doubt your ability to succeed or cope can be such things as:

I hope the bowler doesn't bowl a bouncer!	I'm not good enough!
I can't pick this bowler's wrong'un!	They are too good!
We need to hit some boundaries!	We are losers!
We can't win!	I am a loser!
We will lose!	Woe is me!
I will be dropped!	I am unlucky!
I could be hurt!	They are lucky!

All of the above thought processes will cause the individual to focus on what is happening to them and will prevent them from focusing on the bowler and the ball or on the batter and what type of ball is to be bowled. What needs to happen in this situation is for the individual to recognise the signs of stress and change the thought processes to focus on what needs to be done to achieve a positive outcome. This is where concentration — the ability to focus on what is important at that point in time — comes into its own. If an individual does not have a system of concentration then negative thought processes are likely to ruin many performances. See my routines for concentration on pages 145–152 in chapter 4.

Creating your own cricket world

*Being able to visualise a situation or set of movements is
a large part of being able to do it.*

One of the first test matches I saw was Australia versus England at the Adelaide Oval in the summer of 1958–59. I must have been about ten and it was the last series of the great Australian fast bowler Ray Lindwall. I remember watching Lindwall bowl. What struck me more than anything else, apart from his beautifully balanced action, was that he left imprints on the ground where his feet had landed on his run-up. His feet landed in the identical spot every time he bowled, slowly wearing down the grass and leaving footprints.

I'd never noticed this before, but I think we had gone around to the hill behind the bowler at the northern end of the Adelaide Oval where we could look down on Lindwall running in to bowl. By later in the day, after he'd bowled quite a few overs, the footprints had become very distinct. We left at afternoon tea to catch the last session on television, but I couldn't wait to get home, go to the park and leave footprints of my own on the grass, just like Ray Lindwall. I marked out my run-up and when I ran in to bowl I took great care to tread in the same spot each time. I was far more interested in the footprints than my bowling action or how well I bowled. But the point was, I wasn't just *copying* Ray Lindwall, I was *being* Ray Lindwall. I was creating my own cricket world.

Our make-believe test matches in the backyard, at the park and on the beach were also part of this world. And later in the day, when we'd finished playing outside, we'd be in the house playing dice cricket. It would always be Australia versus England and we'd throw a dice to score runs and take wickets. I played it so much I had books and books full of score cards.

Every couple of years, in winter, the Australian team would tour another country. The most memorable were the tours of England. We'd listen to these on the radio late into the night and I remember having a transistor radio tucked under the pillow in my bed. Years before, my grandfather was a commentator after he finished playing — this was the time before proper radio links between countries. The commentators would sit in the studios in Adelaide where they'd receive cables from the particular cricket ground overseas, for example Lord's in England. The cables gave a very basic description of each ball bowled and the commentators would embellish it, even to the point of tapping a cigar box with a pencil to simulate the bat striking the ball: 'And it's Lindwall coming in now, with that long, loping, beautifully balanced run-up. He's with us now and he bowls [taps box with pencil] and Hutton's back, trying to force it through the covers, but the ever-reliable Harvey swoops on it preventing any thought of a run.' When I listened to the transistor I'd go off to sleep dreaming of Lord's or Old Trafford, or one of the other famous cricket grounds around the world.

By the mid-1950s, when I was listening, there were direct broadcasts, well from England at least, and great commentators such as Allan McGilvray would paint 'word pictures', not only of the ground, but of the atmosphere of the game. These word pictures were so vivid and so well done that, years later, when I went to play at these grounds as a member of the Australian team, they were familiar to me. When I first went to Lords, I felt like I'd been there before. When I first went to the Sydney Cricket Ground I thought I'd been there too. I already 'knew' what the Bradman Stand looked like; I 'knew' what the Ladies Stand and the Members' Stand and the Hill looked like, because of Alan McGilvray and the other commentators of the times.

Visualisation

So this is the way our brains were engaged. We created in our minds a world of test matches, cricket grounds, various conditions and thrilling spectacles —

and every fibre of our being was focused on it. But this creativity and visualisation also had another important benefit. It was an extremely important learning tool in itself, and very important in my overall development as a cricketer. Later in my career I found that I could get just as much value from sitting in my lounge room with my eyes closed visualising batting successfully in a test match as I could actually having a session in the nets. I would visualise batting against Joel Garner, Richard Hadlee, Abdul Qadir and the other great bowlers of the time — whoever we were playing. I would visualise their full repertoire of balls and how I dealt with them successfully. So the make-believe cricket world we had created for ourselves as kids could be applied directly to improving our performances as elite cricketers. This was a fantastic benefit to me in my cricket career. I've said how I could never match the great West Indian batter, Viv Richards, with physical power, but I soon learnt to match him on the scoreboard through the power of my mind.

Watching cricket

We've just discussed how going to the cricket can help you create your very own personal cricket world. But watching cricket has another benefit. Not only does it play a part in developing your creative and visualisation powers, it also helps you develop a feel for the game — its pace, its language and its nuances.

In the early 1990s I coached the Australia A team in a one-day series against Australia and England. We were pretty pleased with ourselves because we had pushed England into third place to make it an all-Australian final. The captain of England then was Mike Atherton, a very good batter. For a few seasons prior to that I'd been a television commentator for Channel 9 and I'd seen Mike captain England on several occasions. When you're a commentator you become, in an imaginary way, the captain of both teams so you can suggest to the audience what you would do with the game in its current position. And I'd noticed from time to time that Mike would miss opportunities that, in my television captain's role, I would have taken. The captain can have a great influence on the game by seizing certain opportunities (seizing the moment) — for example, changing bowlers at a crucial time, setting a certain field to challenge a particular batter — and by just watching and having a feel for the flow of the game. I felt that Mike was missing the odd opportunity here and there, just one or two things each session which could have had an influence on the eventual outcome. And let me say, it's not just Mike: all captains miss opportunities.

I didn't think anything more of it until I was coaching Australia A. One day, at the end of a day's play, Mike came into the Australian players' dressing room and we were having a beer. We were chatting away and he started asking me about some of the blokes I had played with — what sorts of players they were. I remember he asked about Ian Chappell, Doug Walters, Rod Marsh and Dennis Lillee, to name a few. I put his inquisitiveness down to the fact that he was English and hadn't seen much of the Australian cricketers of my era. But then he started asking me about the English players of the time — players like John Edrich, Derek Underwood and Geoff Boycott. These guys were playing for England when he was a kid but he hadn't seen them play. It was then that I realised he hadn't watched a lot of cricket. He had *played* a lot of cricket, there was a lot of organised cricket for kids of his age in England, but he hadn't *watched* a lot of cricket, so he'd missed out on understanding some of the nuances of the game. Suddenly, those questions I had as a commentator were answered.

I have no doubt that I learnt an enormous amount from watching cricket as a kid. There were no commentators to tell you what was going on, you had to watch. When we were younger and Dad was still playing on weekends, we would go and watch him play. Dad would say to us, 'These are the good players in the opposition team, these are the guys you should watch.' Later, we'd go down to the Adelaide Oval and watch the state cricket, and if it was South Australia versus New South Wales, Dad would say, 'Watch the good ones and see how they play the game. Watch Harvey and O'Neil and Benaud and Davidson, they're the best cricketers in that team. Have a good look at what they do.' I didn't think twice about his advice. I would sit right on the fence hanging onto the pickets, watching everything that Neil Harvey and Norm O'Neil did. And Dad would say, 'They're not only good batsmen, they're brilliant fielders. Watch how they move.' Both Harvey and O'Neil played baseball for their state, and O'Neil was picked for the Australian baseball team. He was absolutely brilliant; he threw the ball like a bullet, straight over the stumps every time. So I'd follow their every move. If they came off the field I'd follow them up the stairs; if they went down to the nets, I'd follow them there and watch them practise. I couldn't soak up enough of them. Then I'd go home and play a test match with Ian or Trevor — and if I was on my own, I'd throw a ball up against the back wall and Neil Harvey would invariably score one hundred.

That's how I learnt cricket: by watching, playing and 'becoming' the great cricketers of the time. I created my own personal world which taught me to visualise match scenarios and to understand the pace and nuances of the game.

Training and practice

It doesn't matter what standard of cricket you play, or how organised or
disorganised it is — take a strategic approach to practice and you'll be
amazed by the dramatic improvement in your game.

What is the purpose of training and practice? Test yourself before reading any further. Write your answers down on a piece of paper.

What answers did you come up with?

Did you come up with things like:

- Keeping your eye in?

- Having a fitness work-out?

- Getting into the nets and playing attacking shots?

- Bowling as fast or spinning it as far as you can?

- Rolling the arm over?

- Having some fun with your team-mates?

If so, have another think and write down what you *really* believe practice is for. Please think about this carefully.

Here's what I came up with:

- For batters, working on building an innings, building the tempo and scoring runs.

- For bowlers, working on creating a consistent line and length, then using your weaponry to get batters out.

- For fielders and wicket-keepers, catching at different heights and under various conditions.

- Creating simulated match conditions.

- Preparing psychologically for the next match.

- Honing your batting, bowling and fielding skills.

- Dealing with problems and doing remedial work to correct them.

I hope you chose the sorts of things suggested in the second group, because practice is an extremely important aspect of the game. It is very strategic in its purpose and it is there to take you forward and prepare you for the intensity of competition.

It doesn't matter what standard of cricket you play, or how organised or dis-organised it is, take a strategic approach to practice and you'll be amazed by the dramatic improvement in your game.

This is how it works. There are two golden rules for training:

1 Practice and train the way you want to play.

2 Wherever possible, simulate match environments at training.

The nets

To go into the practice nets without engaging the brain is a wasted opportunity. Whether you're batting or bowling, you must go into the nets with a definite plan. It's common sense. Whenever you want to do something in your daily life, even something simple, you decide on a course of action where you start at point A and finish at point B, having successfully completed the action. It might be as simple as making a piece of toast or buying a newspaper. Your brain devises a plan whereby you undertake an action or series of actions to achieve a goal. Think about it. It's true.

A plan

So why do so many cricketers go into the practice nets without a plan of what they want to achieve? It doesn't make sense. You must have a plan to make your training successful.

I used to have a great time batting in the nets because I treated it like a real match. Even though it was only fifteen to twenty minutes, I'd work at building an innings. I would be batting against the top bowlers of the time such as Dennis Lillee, Jeff Thomson, Ashley Mallett and Terry Jenner. I especially liked batting against Ashley because he was so competitive. I'd go in and say, 'Okay, what field have you got?' And Ashley would say, 'There's a slip, backward point, cover, mid-off, mid-on, mid-wicket, bat-pad, and a backward square leg at 45 degrees.' I used to love that bat-pad because it meant that he was serious and we had a real contest on our hands. So Ashley would bowl and if I hit it I'd say, 'That's three,' and Ashley would say, 'No, no, you're gone!' And I'd reply, 'Hang on, I hit it wide of where you said the fielder was!' So we'd have these full-on arguments about whether he'd got me out or whether I'd scored runs. Shades of the backyard. The same would happen with Dennis Lillee. I'd ask him, 'What's your field?' And he'd say, 'Three slips and a gully,' meaning I should know the rest. So if I nicked one to second slip it was out. It wasn't a matter of 'Oh, that was just a nick that hit the back of the nets.' It was out.

This sort of training was 'real practice' that prepared me for match situations.

My plan

When I went into the nets, the first ten minutes would be like the first twenty minutes of my innings. I would watch the ball and really play every ball on its merits, just like I would in a match. I didn't want to make any mistakes because if I did I would probably be out. For the next few minutes I'd still be playing each ball on its merits, but I would be trying to build the tempo, and for the last five I'd go for my shots. I would still be playing each ball on its merits, but I would be intent on scoring runs more quickly.

Bowlers

Of course, the same applies to bowlers. If you're a fast bowler, you don't steam in first ball and try to bowl flat out; neither do you take it easy and bowl medium pace for the session. You work up to your normal pace, getting your rhythm right, your line and length right, and then working at ways to get the batter out.

Making it count

For the whole of my test career I would bat in the nets for a maximum of fifteen or twenty minutes twice a week. Admittedly, we might practise a little more when we were on tour, but during summer in Australia fifteen minutes twice a week was it. And you know, I never felt the need for more. Why was that? Because for every fraction of every second of that fifteen or twenty minutes all my senses were working on full alert; I was playing a test match, plus I had thought long and hard about it before I went to training. I had a plan and I was prepared. So I always looked forward to practice because I really wanted to keep working on improving my cricket and knew what I wanted to get out of it.

Practice for the game

There are cricketers who go through their whole career never understanding what practice is about. They think they are just going into the nets to play as many shots as they can in fifteen minutes: 'Gee, I've only got fifteen minutes, I'd better go for it.' But if this is the way they're practising, what happens when they go into a game? They either play a lot of shots from the outset or they have to change their whole mental process to do something different. So it's imperative that you practice on Tuesday and Thursday what you intend to do on Saturday, otherwise it's not going to work.

The unplanned approach was the training scenario at South Australia when I started there as coach. Most of the guys would go into the nets and play as many shots as they could; or, if they were bowlers, they would bowl a never-ending over of deliveries with a minimum of thought. The batters nicked balls regularly and got out five or six times in a session. To me this was shocking because I would hate getting out five or six times in a season! Even worse, they thought they were doing well. When I asked them what they were doing they'd reply, 'Practising my shots.' So I'd ask, 'But what about practising not getting out?' They'd look at me blankly. They'd never really thought about why they were there and what they wanted to achieve — they weren't thinking like they would in a game. They hadn't thought about setting the foundations of an innings and gradually building up the tempo; or getting their rhythm, line and length, and working on the batter's weaknesses.

Preparation for match conditions

I began net sessions by asking the question, 'What's the most important part of an innings?' And the guys would reply uncertainly, 'Oh, I suppose the start of it.' And I would ask, 'What else?' The answer is preparation; and we would discuss how preparation for the next time you bat or bowl should start immediately the current innings is over. That means when you go into the nets it is part of your preparation for the next innings or game. Therefore, before going into the nets it's important to get yourself mentally prepared — you get into the right frame of mind. Then it's important to replicate how you would play in that forthcoming match. If you're a bowler you would get your rhythm, line and length first before trying to do too much with the ball. If you're a batter you would take care to become accustomed to the light and the bounce of the pitch, watch every ball and gradually build your innings.

So, under the Chappell regime, everyone in the South Australian squad had to plan their practice sessions to prepare themselves for the next match. We developed this process over time because some of the guys couldn't visualise the match scenario very well, so we refined it, making it better as we went along. One of the problems we had early on was getting the guys to understand that, in normal net practice, you can't work on specific shots. So when a guy was about to go into the nets I would often ask him what he was planning to do. I did this for two reasons. The first was to make sure he had a plan and was clear about what he was trying to achieve. The second was so that, as coach, I could keep an eye on him and see if he was achieving his goals. Often they would answer something like, 'I'm going to work on my cover drives.' And I would reply, 'How are you going to work on your cover drives if the bowlers don't pitch them up outside the off stump?' 'I don't know.' 'You'd better think about it, because if they don't bowl you any balls to hit through the covers, you shouldn't be playing any cover drives, which is the same as in a match. You should be playing other shots.' A normal net session is not where you work on specific weaknesses or problems, it is where you prepare for match conditions. If you want to work on a specific aspect of your game it should be organised separately — that's remedial work.

Every time a player went into the nets we had a rule, just like the game I played with Dennis Lillee, Jeff Thomson, Ashley Mallet and Terry Jenner. The bowlers had to tell the batters what the field was, and they had to start working with each other to decide whether they'd scored runs, there was no run, or they were out. Gradually we helped them develop the feeling of intensity that would occur during a game. Their brains became engaged and they started getting a lot more out of their net sessions, plus a steady improvement in their match play.

> **WIDE NETS — A BONUS**
>
> The narrowness of practice nets can be very inhibiting. That's why I recommend that whenever it is possible position your practice nets to create a much wider corridor. This allows far more space for cutting and hooking and you can even place targets in the nets — a great way to develop a natural style and your run-scoring ability. So, if you're a coach or a player and have the opportunity to decide on the width of your nets, make them at least twice as wide as the conventional design we see around our schools and parks. It will help you create a better practice and learning environment for yourself and your teams.

Training using simulated game sessions

One of the major problems in the modern learning and training environment is that the fundamentals of the game are not being learnt and practised: 'scoring runs' and 'getting wickets' in a competitive environment. You were probably looking for something complicated, but it's that simple. That's what cricket is all about. Now, an unplanned practice session that doesn't stimulate or replicate on-field tension and competitiveness is not working towards those goals. Players need to train to play.

Competitive match pressure

Many players, while hitting and bowling the ball very competently, have not learnt to score runs and get the opposition out. That's why practice and training should as often as possible be relevant to competitive match situations. Practice should be creative and fun. You've read how I'm a great advocate of simulated match-pressure situations in the nets. But I'm an even greater advocate of getting practice sessions out of the nets whenever possible and creating simulated match sessions on the field. More than one net session per week is unnecessary — the real training process comes from creating match play situations.

Short-form games

No practice format will ever completely replicate the tension and competitiveness of a real game, but by being creative we can move a long way towards it. You don't have to play whole matches at training, nor would there be time. The secret is to play sections of a game, or devise short-form games (especially applicable to the one-day format). Here's an example. For many years the Australian team appeared vulnerable when chasing even a meagre total in the fourth innings of a match. I'm sure many teams all over the world have this problem. Here's a way of solving it. Create a match simulation where your team has 100 runs to get. It's the last session of the match, with two hours left to play. Both teams have a chance to win.

This is such an easy scenario for a coach to organise. Anyone can do it. It takes thirteen to play — eleven on the fielding side and two batters. The coach is the umpire, which is a good central position from which to run the session. But once the scenario has been created, it's important that everyone treats it seriously, as they would a real game. The batters in the team really have something to prove — they are the ones normally under pressure in this situation. So it's very beneficial for them. And for the bowlers, they get the opportunity to apply the kind of pressure needed to win in these situations. It's a scenario that can be repeated regularly until the problem improves. In fact you'll find that in most instances it will lift the team's performance generally.

THREE SIMULATED PRACTICE SCENARIOS FOR THE LONG-FORM GAME

- It's the last day of the match. The wicket is worn and playing tricks. Your team has 120 runs to make in the last innings. What's your strategy? Put it into action and win the game.

- The opposition is in a commanding position. We have bowled them out, but we have to survive for 20 overs on a seaming wicket in order to draw the game.

- It's the first morning of the game and we're in the field. We've worked through our game plan and we know that if we work together to put pressure on the batting side, we should be in a good position at lunch. Maximise bowling and fielding opportunities to make every post a winner.

Plus: Try to devise match scenarios tailored to your team.

FOUR SIMULATED PRACTICE SCENARIOS FOR THE ONE-DAY GAME

- Bad weather has shortened the duration of the game. The opposition, our main competitor for the championship, has 120 to make in 20 overs. Our aim is to get them out or stop them scoring. What is our strategy and how will we win? We can't afford one mistake in the field. Let's go.

- There are 15 overs to go. We have to score 9 runs an over (135) to win.

- We've had a very good start, but we're chasing a big score so we have to be careful about losing wickets. Chase the target without hitting the ball in the air.

- The batting team is picking up regular singles and twos. We need to reduce the easy runs. What do we do? Let's put it into action.

Plus: Try to devise match scenarios tailored to your team.

So instead of spending two hours in the nets try spending two hours in a simulated match situation using the whole ground. I've included a few ideas for both the long-form and one-day formats, but with a little thought you can devise match scenarios specifically for your team. You might find that the players are a bit self-conscious the first couple of times, but I've always found that they react very well to these simulated training sessions. It's more fun than the nets, it arouses their competitive instincts so they start thinking in match-mode, and I've always observed improvements in their general game.

COACHING SCHEDULES

For a team that trains three times per week:

One session for basic drills and net practice and two sessions of simulated games or even a real game.

For a team that trains twice a week:

One net session and one simulated session, or operate on my general ratio of one net session to two training sessions, which means that some weeks both your sessions will be simulated match situations.

For a team that trains once a week:

Alternate week-about between net practice and simulated training sessions.

How different is my approach to the conventional one? From the resources angle it's not very different at all — it uses the same training resources available to any team. It is how the resources are used that is the big difference. And when you think about it, it's common sense. We can't expect players to train in one type of environment during the week and then go out and succeed in another type of environment on the weekend. I'll repeat the analogy made before: you can't go from a kindergarten environment at practice to a university environment in a match. It's critical that players train for the competitive match environment. So I encourage all players, coaches and administrators to move their training approach away from the structured, technical and unengaged environment of traditional net practice to the unstructured, creative and switched-on environment of visualisation and simulated match training. It's really taking my own learning and training environment of imaginary test matches in the backyard, at the park and on the beach and moving it into the modern age.

Remember the golden rules of training:

1 Practise and train the way you want to play.

2 Wherever possible, simulate a match environment at training.

3 If what you're doing isn't productive, take a break or try another activity.

Junior learning and training

Simplify the basics of batting for young cricketers.

Over the years of playing, coaching and watching cricket, I have thought a lot about the art of batting and how to simplify its learning for budding young cricketers.

My concern is that many coaches complicate the game in the minds of young people who are just starting out in their cricket life. Batting must seem so complicated to these youngsters; it is no wonder that they think the better batters have found a short-cut to success. In some ways they have, but on the whole they have learnt the fundamentals and have practised long and hard until they have achieved a high level of proficiency.

Comfort, balance and grip

Comfort and balance are two essential ingredients to being able to play well, so the grip and stance are very important.

Getting the right grip. The 'V' of the top hand points towards the splice of the bat, or slightly to the off-side of the splice, to allow for comfortable and natural cocking of the wrist. The bottom hand should be a light grip involving the thumb and forefinger of the bottom hand or the tips of the fingers.

GRIP — TOP-HAND The correct grip is one that allows for a top-hand initiation of the back-lift. It is preferable that the top hand grips the bat at the top of the handle with the 'V' formed by the thumb and forefinger pointing down to the splice of the bat (where the handle joins the bat) to allow for a comfortable and natural cocking of the wrist. Alternatively, it can be angled slightly to the off side of the splice. The important thing is that the blade of the bat should be slightly open to the off side in the back-lift.

GRIP — BOTTOM-HAND Then place the bottom hand on the bat in a comfortable and compatible position. The bottom hand should be a light grip involving the thumb and forefinger of the bottom hand or the tips of the fingers. A firm bottom-hand grip utilising all of the fingers is one of the most destructive things a player can do to prevent a natural back-lift and smooth bat-swing.

STANCE The correct stance is best achieved by standing in a relaxed manner with the body approximately at right-angles to the direction from which the bowler is approaching. The feet should be a comfortable distance apart, knees slightly bent, and the bat placed near the toes of the back foot. A slightly open stance is preferable to a closed stance. As the bowler bowls the ball the batter needs to be in a position to load one leg or the other to initiate the unweighting movement.

Your stance should be relaxed, your body approximately at right-angles to the direction from which the bowler is approaching. The feet are a comfortable distance apart, knees slightly bent, and the bat placed near the toes of the back foot. Adjust slightly to make sure you are comfortable and perfectly balanced to be able to load one leg to initiate the unweighting movement.

Watch the ball and move towards it

With the grip and stance perfected, the two most important things a young batter will ever learn is to *watch the ball* and *intend to move towards the ball* whenever possible.

Focus on the ball

It may seem obvious that you must watch the ball, but I believe many batters only look roughly in the general direction of the ball. Instead, you should be like a movie camera and zoom in to have your whole focus on the ball as it leaves the bowler's hand. All information on the delivery — line and length, spin or swing — is available to the brain the instant the ball leaves the bowler's hand. If you do not have your whole focus on the ball at that stage you may miss some vital information. The other aspect that I found critical was watching the bowler's face as he ran up to the wicket. I picked up a lot of information from his facial expression, but more importantly my peripheral vision picked up vital information from the bowler's body language as he ran to the wicket and prepared to deliver the ball. At this point my focus went to where the ball was going to leave his hand. This was useful from three points of view. One, it allowed me to pick up vital clues; two, it allowed me to easily shift my focus to where the ball was going to leave the bowler's hand; and three, watching the ball as the bowler runs in is extremely fatiguing.

Move toward the ball

By intending to move towards the ball, a batter is going to be in a positive frame of mind and this will cause the brain to prepare the body to unweight appropriately into the active neutral position. This mindset and body position is vital to your ability to track the ball from the bowler's hand. Too many players have deficient footwork because of a negative frame of mind — usually brought about by anxiety or fear — which manifests itself in a significant commitment to either the front or back foot *before* the ball is bowled. This either limits or prevents further footwork once the ball is bowled. This significant commitment triggers the delivery of the bat back into the ball early, and because you stop tracking the ball at this point you miss vital information, such as spin or swing.

The overwhelming majority of the best players in the past fifty years have unweighted by loading the back foot to be able to move forward to as many balls as possible. The reason this proves so effective is that the first point of release by the bowler will indicate a full delivery so it prepares the batter to be able to go forward to the full ball. Should the release point be late the ball will be short, allowing time to plant (and load) the front foot to push back for the short ball. If you prepare for the short ball by unweighting onto the front foot there is not as much time to change direction to go forward should the ball be released early.

Teaching cricket

I've said before how hard it is to teach cricket — especially to kids. Let me explain why this is so.

BATTING in cricket is a very unnatural process compared to batting or its equivalent in other sports that use bats or racquets and balls, such as tennis, baseball and softball. Cricket is the only sport where you play with a vertical bat close to your body. In other sports the bat or racquet is swung more naturally — at waist height and away from the body.

BOWLING is a similar proposition. Bowlers have their arm locked at the elbow, whereas in other sports the ball is thrown — again a far more natural thing to do. Kids learn to throw things at a really early age. They throw their teddies, their food, whatever they have, and when they get a bit older they throw sand at the beach and rocks in the countryside. Who hasn't tried to make a flat stone skim across a river or lake? It's fun and a natural way for the body to dispatch projectiles.

I'm not advocating 'chuckers' and cross-bat shots. Maybe it is because cricket is such an unnatural game for body movement that many coaches feel the need to *teach* it and *drill* it until the cricketer is 'fine-tuned' and has a so-called 'perfect style'.

In South Australia, not only was I in charge of the Redbacks squad; I was also responsible for training and development in the whole elite program — from six-year-old kids to test players like Greg Blewett, Jason Gillespie and Darren Lehmann. A lot of what we were doing was good, but it was 100 per cent structured. Kids of six or seven years old would come to the Adelaide Oval for school holiday clinics. The better ones went into our elite programs and were invited to play in primary school teams and at clubs in the Under 12s, 14s, 16s and 18s. But their only contact with cricket was the practice nets or a game. It wasn't terribly exciting and it wasn't a lot of fun. There wasn't much flair; everyone was so 'correct' and serious, and I became worried that we were turning out robots. There was none of the creative play that we had as kids; none of the freedom that my sons had to learn their skills — hitting targets. And there was none of the freedom Doug Walters, Don Bradman, the Waugh brothers, Glenn McGrath, Adam Gilchrist and Ricky Ponting had when they learnt to play. Bradman, in fact, is the perfect example. He grew up in the country with no one to play with and hardly played any organised cricket until he was a teenager.

Creative play

Here's an interesting aside. In China, the home of table tennis, they also identify talented young kids and bring them into elite programs. But they don't let them play a match for some time. They take them through the basics, they get them to have fun and play tricks with the bat until they can do almost anything before they let them play in tournaments. It's creative and unstructured. By comparison, when I look at our junior cricket programs in Australia, the kids are just getting technical tuition in the nets, with a match on weekends. If our coaching programs become like machines churning out sausages, then Australian cricket will be the loser for generations. Being a former Australian captain and passionate about this wonderful sport, it is pretty hard to take.

My priority is to create an environment that allows kids' natural style and enthusiasm to shine through, and that allows them to learn and deal with competitive stress. It must be fun.

These formative ideas tried out in Adelaide have been further developed to form the basic learning philosophy that we've called the Chappellway:

> To create an environment where kids can learn to play intuitively, where they learn aspects of the game subconsciously while having fun, ideally from a very early age — from the time they first pick up a bat and ball. Research by experts such as Professor Bruce Abernethy of the University of Queensland suggests that the first 100 hours of contact with a new activity is critical to the learning process.

By taking this approach we believe both kids and adults have the best chance of maximising their potential and becoming exciting players — players who are entertaining to watch. So it's not only the players who benefit, it's the spectators as well.

Intuitive learning

Here are two more golden rules, this time on learning:

1 Intuitive learning through a creative and unstructured environment produces exciting cricketers.

2 Intuitive learning occurs more easily in an unstructured environment than a structured environment because it reduces anxiety and unproductive stress, and allows the subconscious to control movement.

Intuitive cricketers, players with flair such as Sachin Tendulkar, Ricky Ponting, Adam Gilchrist and Brian Lara, not only make a lot of runs for their team, but are also exciting to watch. They play shots and their run rates are usually high. And the great bowlers are the same, for example Shane Warne, Muttiah Muralitharan and Shoaib Akhtar. They bowl with great intuition and flair — there is always something happening. It was the same with the great bowlers I played with and against: Dennis Lillee, Richard Hadlee and Michael Holding.

When kids come along to our cricket clinics these are the things we need to bear in mind. What sort of cricketers do we want to produce and how do we best achieve this? By using the concepts I've detailed here as part of the grounding for our young players, we have a better chance of developing the Adam Gilchrists, Ricky Pontings, Shane Warnes and Jason Gillespies of the future. But if we continue with our structured clinical environment we are going to produce a lot of one-dimensional players. Their growth will be stunted and they will never reach their full potential. I think about this every time I see a group of young kids at a coaching clinic.

Technique

Do you find the unstructured, intuitive approach risky? If you do I guess you see less risk in learning through the structured way. But when I look back on it, unstructured learning was actually the best way to develop technical skills. That was the beauty of what our father did for us. Lynn Fuller taught us how to stay in and Dad taught us how to bat, how to make runs. At the risk of being repetitive, making runs and taking wickets is what the game is all about. We have to play with kids like I did with my son Jonathan on the tennis court: teach them to be creative and have some fun. Then as they get older we can help tighten up their technique a little bit, just as I did with Jason Gillespie. We didn't change his style or what type of cricketer he wanted to be, we just helped him become more efficient and less prone to injury. It's a similar scenario for kids who grow up in the country, as so many of our great cricketers have done. They learn to play the game their way, then when they arrive at a city club their technique might be polished up a little bit. That's a far more efficient way for them to learn and develop.

Confidence

We've got to be very careful with kids coming into the game. If we try to teach them by rote, we are likely to destroy their confidence and a lot of kids will lose interest in the game. We've got to add more dimensions. We've got to stop *teaching* them how to play and instead create an environment where they can *learn* how to play. It's like the title of the movie *Back to the Future*. We need to draw on the intuitive learning of the past to take us into the future. We need to get 'back to the future' with our kids.

LEARNING GAMES FOR KIDS

BOWLING COMPETITION

This is a great exercise for helping you to bowl straight. You can play it on your own, with a couple of friends or in a more organised way at training. The aim is to see who hits the stumps the most times. If you're on your own you can see what you can score out of ten — and next time see if you do better. But let's say we're at training. The coach splits the squad into groups of five or six. Each group has a ball and plays in a separate net. Each player gets to bowl (say) six balls. The near misses cause a lot of excitement, but the tension is really on when two players are tied with one ball to go! Playing in different conditions and with different balls is also very beneficial because it helps young players learn about the different bounce, and how they have to change their approach to reap the best results.

BATTING TARGETS

Set up some targets, say 10-20 metres from the bat, and allot points to them. Throw a set number of balls to the batter — they can be underarm, overarm or a bowl. Points are awarded for hitting the targets.

FIELDING COMPETITION

Similar to the bowling, set up different targets at different heights and locations. Allocate points for each target and have some fun competitions.

With catching, use slips catching cradles or rollers to create fun environments and enjoy some competitive training. (See more about this on pages 203–204 of chapter 5.

Another beneficial form of catching training is 'conceptual interference' where the use of a variety of balls from different angles stimulates the subconscious brain to deal with a variety of situations to promote natural learning.

These sorts of fun competitions can be used at any level of cricket.

Training for batting

The principal concept of batting is an understanding of the role of stimulus and response. Batting is always a response (reaction) to the ball that's been bowled (the stimulus).

In training and coaching sessions, creating stimuli similar to those that batters will experience in the competitive arena is crucial to their development and preparation. In the sports science community this form of training is called 'specificity'.

SPECIFICITY means you train specifically for the task at hand. Here's an example. Let's say we want to increase the team's aerobic capacity for running between wickets. A non-specific training exercise would be sprint training to gain extra aerobic capacity and sharpness in running. The team turns out wearing shorts, T-shirts and training shoes and the players run a series of sprints. But sprints don't simulate what it's like to run with pads, rib pads, an arm-guard, helmet, and box, and carrying a bat. Running with pads on is far more difficult and exhausting. Under the specificity theory the coach would have two batters fully geared up on a pitch running a series of singles, twos, threes and fours. In other words you are extending your aerobic capacity while practising the actual task or discipline. It has obvious benefits over non-specific training and can be applied to strength-building, concentration, movement and in fact every aspect of the game.

NON-SPECIFICITY is using another sport or discipline to train for a specific area of your sport — in this case, cricket. Weight sessions in the gym, jogging, swimming, hand–eye coordination exercises and sports like golf and baseball are all examples of non-specificity. So what are the benefits of non-specificity and why is it used? Non-specific training has two roles:

- to allow for rest and recuperation;
- to assist in the process of changing deeply ingrained movement patterns.

Cricketers have traditionally used golf for relaxation, but golf can also be a good way of understanding body movement. For example, a coach could use the golf-swing to help players understand body movement that occurs when driving a cricket ball. A different environment gives the batter an opportunity to relax and experience the movement from a learner's perspective. Finding an activity to which the player hasn't had much exposure can be extremely beneficial. However, while there are benefits, in the end the learning from that activity needs to be reincorporated back into the specific cricket skill — in this case driving — for players to gain maximum benefit. Ultimately maximum learning is achieved by batting in a competitive environment and building a large memory bank of batting responses.

Part-training

Another well-used training technique is 'part-training'. Part-training splits batting up into its various components and rehearses them one by one. An example is practising getting to the pitch of ball. In this case the ball would be thrown over and over, while the batter moves their front foot to the ball, but does not hit the ball. Only part of the batting action is completed. This can be particularly useful for fine-tuning stroke-play or for remedial work where the coach and player are correcting a problem. But I believe a batter gets far more benefit from getting the key movements of unweighting, coiling, using levers and timing correct, and training in a simulated match situation similar to what they would face in the competitive environment.

Drills

In the 1990s the sporting community became fascinated by drills, which have been promoted as effective ways to learn and refine movement patterns. Over the years batters have used 'ball in a sock' drills to practise their movements. A ball in a sock or stocking is hung from the ceiling or overhead beam. Once the batter hits the ball the first time it swings back in a different direction, to which they have to respond. It has proven to be a good way to expose young players to what movement feels like. More dubious in terms of their benefits are 'dropping-ball' drills and 'underarm' drills. In the dropping-ball drill the coach or a player stands just to the off side of the batter and drops the ball for them to hit. The idea is that the batter learns fast movement of the hands. The underarm drill involves bowling the ball along the ground with the aim of training bat-swing. Drills can be beneficial, especially when the player is new to the game or when the drill is new to an experienced player. However, it should always be remembered that drills are tools, not an end in themselves. To be of real benefit they must always be reincorporated back into the whole action of batting.

MAKING THE ON-DRIVE EASY

It's generally recognised that the hardest shots to play are the on-drive and straight drive. Batters seem to get tangled up, they get the pads and body in the way and they get themselves off balance. But here's a great drill that will put you right. My assistant coach at the Redbacks, Tim Nielsen, was also the assistant coach on the Australian tour of the West Indies in 2003, where he introduced the drill to Ricky Ponting. Ricky quickly recognised the balance, control and fluidity it gave him.

AIM: To improve balance, footwork, body position and bat-swing of senior or advanced cricketers.

METHOD: The bowler throws balls on a full length, varying them from outside the off stump to leg stump.

BATTER: The batter makes a full step to the ball, keeping the ball on the off side of the leading foot, no matter whether the ball is pitched on the off side, straight or on the leg side. By keeping the ball to the off side of the leading foot the batter takes the head to the line of the ball, thus maintaining the best position for balance and bat-swing. This is particularly important when the ball is pitched straight or on leg stump. The tendency here is to take the leg to the line of the ball and the head to the off side of the line, causing the batter to overbalance and the leading leg to interfere with the bat-swing. Balance and bat-swing are affected by the position of the front foot. Because the knee bends over the foot, it is important that the batter point the toe in the general direction of the intended drive. This will keep the batter balanced and will allow the knee to flex in the direction of the shot, preventing the knee from getting in the way of the bat-swing. So what we are doing, in effect, is playing the same front-foot drive, but in various directions. It's a cover drive down the on side.

There are two aspects of this drill to which you should pay special attention:

1 UNWEIGHTING THE BAT

The unweighting of the bat is important because it locks the front shoulder in and coordinates the top half of the body with the bottom half. If done correctly it empowers the top hand to lead into the chosen stroke. As we discussed in 'Unweighting the bat' on pages 17–21 of chapter 1, the correct way to do this is by initiating the movement of the semi-cocking of the wrist with the top hand while only having a light bottom-hand grip. Only the thumb and forefinger of the bottom hand should be used at this point and the toe of the bat should be angled towards first or second slip. A straight back-lift is not natural — it impedes the bat-swing because the bat has to travel around the body during the stroke, and it prevents the body loading correctly.

2 THE FRONT-FOOT STRIDE

Placing the emphasis on the stride delays the movement of the hands and arms. By delaying the hands and arms, timing and power are increased. Conversely, if the stride is too short or the hands and arms begin to move too early, which will shorten the stride anyway, timing and power will be adversely affected, along with balance.

One area of drilling that I do not recommend is the use of drills to speed up movement patterns. The 'dropping-ball drill' mentioned above is one of these. The idea is that such drills develop speed and power. But what actually happens in a lot of cases is that players start to speed up their hands without a corresponding increase in the other body parts that are crucial to the use of levers and timing. In fact, it has the effect of changing the internal timing mechanisms for that movement, which becomes very hard to change — as golfers around the world appreciate.

Here's a golden rule on power:

> Power is achieved by the appropriate response to stimulus and the body parts working together to achieve the desired outcome. The whole movement creates acceleration through the ball.

As coaches we should always help batters develop whole body movements. Power will come from gradual exposure to greater stimuli and the demand for better results. Specificity — training to react effectively to stimulus in the match-simulated environment — is the answer.

Training for bowling

The great thing about bowling is that it initiates the action. By initiating the action it draws a response from the batter. The fact that the bowler initiates the play is the primary concept that needs to be understood above everything else.

Remember how the batter reacts to stimuli? Well, those stimuli are provided by the bowler. Bowling has three fundamentals:

1 a reproducible action;

2 a strategy, that is, a number of deceptive ploys to manipulate the batter into making mistakes; and

3 an acceptance that a batter's response is not in the bowler's control. (Sometimes they play great shots!)

Each of these fundamentals needs to be learnt, developed and trained. However, like batting, it is crucial that they are incorporated into the whole art of bowling. This is a very important point that often gets lost in coaching and training.

Consistency

The reproducible action is very important because it creates a pattern of *consistency*. Creating a pattern of consistency for the batter is the first step in getting them out. Batters have different strengths and habits, so the key is to recognise what these are, then coerce the batter into responding consistently to your bowling. For this you need a *reproducible action* — you need to be able to control where the ball is bowled. Once you've gained that consistent response you can manipulate it using your 'bowling weaponry' such as line, length, swing, seam, flight and spin — this is your *strategy*. In creating the consistent response, and in using your weaponry, you'll be hit for runs. But that's okay because bowlers can't control *the batter's response* — once the ball is bowled you have no control over where it is hit. This is a key bowling attitude that needs to be understood and learnt.

Glenn McGrath is an expert at this approach. He bowls a very consistent line and length. For example, after doing his homework on a particular batter Glenn might decide to bowl a good length just outside the off stump. The batter gets into the habit of moving forward and hitting the ball into the covers. He might even get one through the off-side field for some runs. But then Glenn might bowl one a tiny bit shorter or one that moves away a little bit more off the seam. The batter, lulled into a false sense of security by the previous balls, moves forward again, but this time he is not quite to the pitch or the line of the ball. One mistake is often all that it takes to send him back to the shed.

Using your memory bank

There is another important addition to bowling strategy besides weaponry, and I alluded to it before in the example of Glenn McGrath. It's your knowledge of the different situations you find yourself in and the different batters you bowl against. In the past, most people have referred to this knowledge as 'experience'. But I prefer to call it the 'memory bank'. The bowler's memory bank is filled with thousands of 'files' about all the different match situations they've been in, all the different pitches they've played on, and all the batters they've bowled against. Good bowlers constantly draw on their memory bank to get wickets — it's a key part of their strategic thinking.

These are the fundamentals of bowling — simple, effective, fun and exciting. In fact, I've coached cricketers who were never that interested in bowling, but once they understood these fundamentals it became fun and took on a whole new meaning for them. They became really excited about it. And the more good bowlers your team can draw on, the stronger the team.

Practice nets

Training is the perfect place for bowlers to develop these fundamentals and enhance their skills. Unlike batting, where the nets can inhibit the learning process, for bowlers the nets are like a fantastic learning laboratory. Here you can work on your consistency and weaponry — speed and swing, cut and different pitches, spin and wind, different batters and their reactions — and you can hone your attitude to the batter's response. You can work out with many different batters in lots of different conditions, so you can build up your memory bank of strategies, which can then be reapplied in a match. So it's crucial to create a training environment where all this can take place, which is why I keep emphasising the use of visualisation and the simulated match scenario at training. It's the only effective way to develop strategies and experiences that are relevant to the match situation. Every time a bowler goes into the nets they can set up a match simulation. Treat it as if you're bowling an over in a match — six balls. Look for your consistency and then use your weaponry to get the batter out. If there are no batters about, try bowling to a wicket-keeper, or simply grab a bucket of balls and practise by yourself. And don't forget the targets!

BOWLING DRILLS

Batting and fielding have been swamped with drills that split whole movements and actions into parts, and train those sections separately. I don't agree with many of these methods and, as you've read, I believe it's crucial that we come from the angle of the complete movement. However, there are some drills that benefit various parts (or positions) in the bowling action — provided they are incorporated back into the whole movement and the simulated match situation.

ONE OVER ON, ONE OVER OFF — JUST LIKE A GAME

Here's a great way of training in the nets. Imagine you're bowling in a match. Tell the batter your field, then bowl a six-ball over. Hand the ball over to a team-mate to bowl an over and do some fielding practice or other exercise such as push-ups and sit-ups while they're bowling their six balls. Then go back and bowl another over. Bowl as many overs as either the training session will allow or you would normally bowl in a spell, concentrating on consistency, strategy and your attitude to the batter's response.

CORE STRENGTHENING

A strong core — the muscles of the mid-section of the body that joins the top half to the bottom half — is very important in bowling. The main muscle groups are those of the stomach and the lower back. These help keep the spine aligned and share the workload in the coiling process when the body winds up to store power for the delivery. A good exercise is sit-ups using a medicine ball. Two team-mates lie feet-to-feet on the ground, knees bent to about 30 degrees. One throws the ball so the other catches it as they move back from the upright position to the lying position. They then return the throw as they return to the seated position. Do this exercise between overs at training.

Medicine ball sit-ups are a great way to strengthen your core muscles for bowling. Make sure you follow this exercise by immediately going into a bowling session so the brain applies the strengthening exercise to the relevant muscles. Watch out for signs of fatigue the key is to not over stress the body.

Bowling weaponry – swing, swerve, spin and deception

The bowler's weapons are swing, swerve, cut, spin and speed variation.

Swing

A cricket ball moving through the air causes the air to separate from its sides. Typically, this layer of air, called the *boundary layer*, occurs about half way round the ball. Swing and swerve depend on the air layer leaving the ball a little earlier or later on one side than the other. From a shiny surface it leaves early, from a slightly rough surface it leaves late, and from a very rough surface it leaves somewhere between the two. Pointing the seam to one side is the equivalent of changing the roughness of that side. Different atmospheric conditions such as humidity and wind can also assist swing.

Just to confuse matters, the ball can also swing *away* from the rougher side! This is called *reverse swing*. When one side of the ball gets very rough the air leaves it earlier than the side of the ball which is only moderately rough. Therefore, if a ball is worn, a bowler can increase this roughness using the seam, resulting in the ball leaving the very rough side earlier than the moderately rough side. So the ball then swings in 'reverse'.

Outswinger

The *outswinger* is the key weapon in the fast bowler's arsenal. It creates opportunities for catches behind the wicket as the batter commits to the drive, especially when the ball swings late in flight. Outswing occurs when the layer of air leaves the off side of the ball slightly later than the leg side, and the ball curves to the off. The bowler should hold the ball so the seam points towards the slip area. The exact amount of angle will depend on the airflow and direction. You need to vary seam direction as well as speed to find the right balance for achieving swing. As the ball gets older, keeping one side of the ball shiny assists swing.

Inswinger

The *inswinger* is also a potent weapon. It's the opposite of an *outswinger* so you need to have the seam facing towards leg slip and the rough side of the ball to the leg side. The key is to achieve a consistent wrist release point that allows the ball to maintain a consistent seam angle. Opening up your action at release, positioning the wrist towards the leg side and angling the delivery into the batter can all assist the *inswing*.

Swerve, cut and spin

Spin and swerve, which is also known as the 'Magnus Effect', occurs in all ball sports. Golf is a good example. Hitting across or outside the ball puts a side-spin on it, causing the infamous slice and hook. Tennis is another good example — players use topspin to make the ball drop quickly. This 'swerving' of the ball is a result of spin. Spinning a ball causes air to cling longer to one side of the ball than the other. But unlike swing, where the air is separated by roughness, swerve is a result of the opposite sides of the ball spinning at different speeds against the oncoming air. For example, a top-spinner has the top surface of the ball moving faster against the oncoming air than the bottom, which is moving *with* the air. This creates resistance at the top of the ball and it 'swerves' downwards.

If the friction between the ball and the pitch is adequate, and there is rotation on the ball, deviation will result. This deviation is known as 'cut' in fast–medium bowling, and 'turn' in spin bowling.

The amount of rotation that is generated on the ball is determined by the wrist action and the grip. Holding the ball across the seam, with a wide gap between the fingers and rotating the wrist around the joint, will deliver the most rotation to the ball. However, in fast and medium-pace bowling, this often results in such a significant change in pace it becomes ineffective. Therefore, unless the wicket is soft and it is advantageous to slow down your pace and use cut as a deceptive tool like a spin bowler, then it's better to grip the ball so the delivery can be bowled at pace:

- *Off-cutter* — Grip the ball with the index finger on the seam pointing towards the slips. At the point of delivery rotate under and down the leg side of the ball.

- *Leg-cutter* — Grip the ball with the middle finger on the seam rotating across the top and down the side of the ball.

The slower ball

Because the fingers move across the ball upon release, cutters have the effect of becoming slightly slower than balls that are bowled as swing, offering another important tool of deception for fast and medium-pace bowlers. There are several methods of bowling the slower ball:

- by decreasing the amount of wrist work. This has the effect of the ball hovering towards the batsman, but requires considerable practise.

- by changing the position of the ball in the hand. This can change the pace of the ball at release.

All the slower ball methods need regular practice as the key is to bowl them with the same action.

Spin

There are two types of spin bowling: leg-spin and off-spin. Both involve the rotation of the wrist to impart spin on the ball. The fingers assist the wrist, but the key is the wrist set-up.

Leg-spin (or wrist spin) wrist positions:

Leg-spin — the back of the wrist points towards your face.

Top-spin — the back of the wrist points towards the batter.

Wrong'un — the back of the wrist points towards the ground.

Flipper — the back of the wrist rotates towards the umpire.

Zooter — similar position to leg-spin, but the wrist stays on top of the ball through the delivery, causing minimal ball rotation.

Off-spin (or finger spin) finger positions:

Note, the term 'finger spin' is misleading because it implies that this type of bowling relies solely on the fingers to impart rotation on the ball. However, like wrist spin, the rotation of the wrist and the fingers work together to generate spin. The movement or position of the index finger assists us in describing the different deliveries.

Off-spin — the index finger ends up to the leg side of the batter.

Under-spin — the index finger rotates around the ball in an anti-clock-wise motion.

Top-spin — the index finger travels in a semi-circle across the top and to the leg-side of the ball.

Arm ball — similar to an outswinger in pace bowling.

Leg cutter — similar to a leg-cutter in pace bowling where you run your index finger down the off-side of the ball.

Doosra — Muttiah Muralithearan's 'doosra' also breaks from the leg and involves the ball spun by the thumb and index finger with the back of the wrist facing the batter at release. It requires incredible flexibility and mobility.

Specificity — bowling

My approach to learning and training is based on the principle of allowing the body to learn how to respond naturally to stimuli created in the environment. The body works like a spring in a process called the 'kinematic link'. In bowling it means that when the front foot of the delivery stride hits the ground, the forces generated move up through the ankles, knees, hips and spine and out to the arms, where energy is released into the ball. This requires specific movements and specific timing of those movements to generate optimum performance — mostly observed as a fluid, easy action. In other words these movements are bowling specific and do not apply to other sports. Therefore to learn and develop successfully a bowler needs to bowl. Mark Philippoussis didn't learn that serve without serving, Tiger Woods didn't learn that drive without driving and Shane Warne didn't learn his bowling wizardry without bowling.

This notion creates a problem for a lot of elite bowlers whose coaches often curtail the amount of bowling they do at training to prevent wear and tear on the body. Bowlers, they argue, put a lot of stress on their bodies and eventually they wear out. The problem with this argument is that, if you believe in specificity, ultimately bowlers have to bowl in order to improve. By not bowling, they are being prevented from developing consistency, strategies and exposure to understanding different batters' responses. Moreover, they are limiting their exposure to the forces they would experience in a match, and therefore the build-up of experiences in their memory bank.

A WORD FROM 'THE DON' ABOUT SPECIFICITY IN BOWLING

Don Bradman once made an interesting point about a champion footballer, a very fit young guy who came along to cricket practice and bowled a few overs in the nets. Next day he pulled up with muscle soreness. Bradman used this example to demonstrate to his players that you have to train your muscles in the specific activity in which you want them to perform.

Postural integrity

So should bowlers bowl more? And how do we solve the problem of stress on the body? If we can solve the problem of stress there should be no argument.

It is very important that bowlers maintain 'postural integrity' throughout the bowling movement. This way they put less stress on their bodies. Postural integrity means having an aligned spine at two crucial points in the bowling action: when the back foot lands and when the front foot lands. It's at these two points that the body is under most stress because of the high forces created by ground contact. But in the act of bowling the coiling movement to gain power for the delivery 'twists' the spine. This coiling and uncoiling is essential in the bowling action. However, it becomes an issue if the body continues to coil after back-foot landing.

The following three points are important in maintaining spinal integrity:

1 The bowler should have completed the coil at back-foot landing.

2 The hips should have rotated back to the direction of the delivery at ball release.

3 The core muscles of the stomach and lower back should have been conditioned to manage the stresses of coiling and uncoiling through the bowling action.

Coiling as your back foot lands puts incredible pressure on the spine. However, coiling before the back-foot landing, and uncoiling before the front foot lands, is essential.

The core

The core, that part of the body between the upper body and legs, plays a very important part in bowling. It not only maintains the correct relationship between the upper and lower sections of the body, it manages the degree of separation of the angle between the shoulders and hips that is essential to develop the torque (rotational force) required to get the ball down the other end. Many young medium-pace and fast bowlers have insufficient strength in their core muscles to maintain spinal integrity during the bowling action. Not only does this make the young bowler susceptible to injury, it causes inconsistent ball release.

The run-up

In my experience as a coach the most common reason for loss of spinal integrity is a run-up that is too fast or too energetic. What happens is that the bowler creates such momentum through the speed or energy of the run-up that they can't coil properly into the delivery action. Dennis Lillee is one of the most famous examples of this problem. In the early part of his career, Dennis had a tear-away run-up where his elbows splayed outwards a bit like wings. It meant that sometimes he was coiled appropriately into the delivery, but often he wasn't. Eventually, he broke down with a severe back injury that kept him out for eighteen months. Sometime after rehabilitation, Dennis worked with a special running coach to reconfigure his run-up so that his elbows worked appropriately, his spine was aligned, and his speed allowed him to be coiled appropriately when his back foot landed. He worked incredibly hard at this and, as history tells us, he made a tremendous comeback to be one of the great fast bowlers of all time, with one of the most classic bowling actions.

SEEKING EXPERT ADVICE FOR POSTURAL INTEGRITY PROBLEMS

In training, it is important to make sure all bowlers maintain postural integrity. If they are unable to, their problem needs to be corrected as a matter of urgency. Watch for patterns that are not fluid and efficient.

Injury risk

By maintaining postural integrity through appropriate coiling and uncoiling, the bowler can eliminate much of the body stress and injury risk. Postural integrity coupled with the appropriate muscle strength and joint flexibility should keep the bowler relatively free from injury. Here's where non-specific training such as gym work enters the picture. Weights and various other kinds of exercise programs certainly assist in strengthening the relevant muscles. That's why a coach should try to integrate sensible body strengthening and body-flexing work into training sessions as often as possible. For example, a core strengthening exercise such as sit-ups with a medicine ball should be followed immediately with an over in the nets. This is repeated a number of times. What this does is allow the brain to directly apply the strengthening exercise to the specific bowling movement. It also creates a more match-simulated training session because the bowler has one over on, then one over off, and in between has other forms of exertion. The key is to not over stress the body so a light medicine ball is sufficient.

Imbalance

Another concept that has become fashionable with strength trainers is the rebalancing of body imbalance due to one-sided activities. This is an interesting concept, however it is important to note that provided an action is consistent with the movement patterns of the individual, there is a cross-training effect where the opposite muscle groups are trained as well — thanks to the nervous system. I believe it is more important to spend the time optimising the individual's natural movement patterns than correcting muscle imbalances from manufactured movement patterns that are inconsistent with a person's body.

Individuality

This brings me to the concept of 'individuality'. As humans we all have different length bones, muscles, joint spacing and ligament tensions; to expect two bowlers to have the same action is crazy. We can only be what we are and with practice optimise our performance. But around the cricket world coaches change bowlers' actions. In my view there are only two reasons to adjust a bowler's action:

- injury potential caused by a poor run-up and delivery fundamentals;

- inconsistency at ball release due to poor fundamentals.

The young Dennis Lillee in his delivery stride. He suffered from problems with his run-up and subsequent inappropriate body coil.

The latter problem often occurs with young medium-pace bowlers who have insufficient strength, especially in the core muscles. In this situation poor fundamentals are likely.

Some coaches try to increase a young bowler's speed by training them to pull their front arm rapidly into the body, thereby speeding up the bowling arm. Potentially it can achieve this, but if the body isn't in an appropriate position during the delivery stride it will compromise the integrity of the spine, which is dangerous. Trying to manipulate the timing mechanism of the bowling process can create more problems than it solves. Allowing the body to load and unload naturally will optimise the bowler's innate abilities.

Here are two golden rules on training and development:

- Let the young body grow and become strong naturally over time.

- Stimulate the young athlete with a variety of learning experiences and the body will develop to its full potential.

If there is only one concept you learn from this book let it be the concept of the whole body working in natural timing to generate the optimal end result.

Training for fielding and wicket-keeping

Fielding

Fielding is an area of the game that has really improved with the introduction of the one-day game. The accuracy of the throwing, the acrobatics of catching, and sliding to prevent runs and maintain pressure are exciting to watch. Fielding has become so important that the quality of your fielding can determine whether you get picked in the team. It's therefore a very important part of training.

I have been fortunate to see some great fielders in action. Players such as Viv Richards, Clive Lloyd, Mark Waugh and Ricky Ponting instantly come to mind. They all displayed beautiful balance and composure on the field and gave the impression they really enjoyed their fielding. Anyone with average ball skills can become good, efficient fielders; in fact, I have seen ordinary fielders turn themselves into very good fielders with persistent effort and practice. Fielders who treat fielding as a challenge, who create run outs, generate catching opportunities and save precious runs, seem to have a good time too and can ultimately win the game for their team.

The keys to fielding are:
- confidence
- good reflexes and response
- agility and balance
- the ability to throw well.

For players who have achieved a good standard, confidence is the main key. But fielding also requires good responses to stimuli because balls arrive at different speeds and from different angles. Fielders also need flexibility, balance and agility to bend, stretch and extend rapidly to catch and throw the ball. Decisions must be made about how to intercept the ball and which wicket to throw to. And all this must be done without mistakes. No wonder cricketers sometimes lose confidence in their ability to field.

Traditionally, fielding practice has been an adjunct to the core training of batting and bowling. However, in recognition of the effect good fielding can have on the result of a game, it has become increasingly significant in training programs. Like batting and bowling, specificity is the best training and learning method, so training for fielding is most effective when it can simulate a competitive match environment. The training scenarios discussed earlier in this chapter for batting and bowling also offer an opportunity for good fielding practice.

WHEN A FIELDER HAS LOST CONFIDENCE

Confidence is essential to good fielding. But there are always times when a fielder loses their touch and confidence. In such cases the coach can devise a program tailored to restore the confidence of a particular person. For example, the problem might be catching. The coach and player could do some catching work with a tennis ball, then move on to the cricket ball. The key is to make sure that the player tastes success before moving on to the next level of difficulty. Slowly, the player should regain confidence.

Wicket-keeping

Wicket-keeping generates significant forces through the body: firstly, as the person pushes off from the ground, and secondly, as the body absorbs the shock of impact upon landing. To maximise efficiency and reduce the potential for injury, keepers need to train for the movement patterns they use in keeping. These movements include squatting while maintaining appropriate spinal curvature, extending out of the squat using the legs to push into the ground (with a stable core to support the upper body), and diving and lunging (ensuring that the hip joints are the point of extension).

Keepers need to have strong ankles, calves and hamstrings, as a large proportion of their movements extend from the squatting position. Training the rear postural chain of muscles (back, gluteus [buttocks], hamstrings, calves) is very beneficial, especially if it is undertaken in the same timing patterns as in the game situation. It's important too that keepers train to deal with what I call 'disrupted sighting' — which is when the batter moves into the keeper's line of sight while playing the ball. Keepers can practise finding the best position for various bowlers and situations; providing them with as many different situations as possible by changing bowlers, altering the bowler's directions, altering surfaces and changing batters is the best way to develop good, all-round wicket-keepers.

Simulated games

As is the case with batting, one thing that clearly differentiates the better wicket-keepers is that they don't commit too early. It's important, therefore, to practise leaving the decision to move for as long as possible, and there is no better place to develop stimulus and response training than in training situations and game scenarios. Different bowlers present different challenges, and understanding the bowler's mannerisms and different wrist positions assists greatly in correct decision-making. Taking returns is another important skill, and exposure to different throwers from a range of distances is the only way to train for it. Again, the simulated game session is a great place to practise these skills.

Concentration

Unlike other players, wicket-keepers are involved in every ball delivered and the majority of returns for the whole innings. Given that it's impossible to concentrate at full intensity all day, wicket-keepers need to develop routines of concentration. I used a method of three concentration levels that I found very successful and which I discuss fully in chapter 4. In between deliveries I would relax, looking at the crowd or chatting to a team-mate. As soon as the bowler turned into his run I would focus on the bowler's face and body movements, and at delivery this would change to a fierce focus on the ball.

Finally, the wicket-keeper, along with the captain, sets the standard for the emotional behaviour of the team. So it's important in your development to train your system to remain in control and focused on helping to keep the team's emotions under control. While all players can benefit from this discipline, it is a must for keepers. Working with individual team members in situations where their behaviour or attitude isn't helping the rest of the group is a great way to develop these vital life skills.

You can find out more about this in 'Coaching wicket-keeping and fielding', on pages 203–204 of chapter 5.

Remedial work

From time to time, we all need to sort out a glitch in our game. It might be that you've temporarily lost the ability to bowl your outswinger as well as you were earlier in the season, or you might be unbalanced playing on the leg side and hitting the ball in the air too often. These problems not only affect your wicket-taking and run-scoring abilites; they can also have a psychological effect that can spread to other areas of your game. So it's important that you fix the little problems before they become big ones, just as you do with your car.

Here's where remedial work comes into play, and there are three main ways of fixing problems:

- by increasing the range of experiences to stimulate the natural learning process;
- by distraction training — using a conscious thought process to free up the subconscious mind to generate more suitable movement patterns;
- by engaging in various levels of competition.

Often these three methods are combined.

The first, increasing the range of experiences by learning and playing in different conditions, was discussed earlier in this chapter, so I will move on to the second, distraction training.

Distraction training

The object of the exercise here is to divert the conscious thought processes from previously learnt movement patterns. All you nets-fanatics will be glad to hear that this is where the nets come into their own because it is a controlled environment where the coach and player can work on a specific problem. Take, for example, the batter who's having problems defending their wicket. Of course, the coach needs to be creative and understand the requirements and temperaments of different people. But in this instance the coach may extend the width of the stumps and have a session where the goal for the batter is to stop the ball from hitting them. This distracts the batter's attention away from technique — things like foot position, elbow position or back-lift (the micro elements) — to the specific problem of protecting the stumps (the macro element). Using the nets in this way to change stimuli and achieve goals can be effective, fun and induce a sense of achievement in both the player and the coach; it certainly doesn't need to be a dour and solemn occasion.

Levels of competition

The third aspect of remedial treatment is competition. Here's a great example of using competition as part of remedial work. One of our young champion swimmers, just fifteen years old, has been doing some wondrous things and is on the verge of world times. But there's a little glitch in her stroke that is preventing her from moving to the next level. So her coach works through correcting her stroke at training, then it's time to start competition again. But the coach won't let her compete at the level she was at before because she will probably not do as well immediately, and that may affect her confidence. So she will compete at a lower level, which will not only allow her to get used to her new stoke in the stressful environment of competition, but also allow her to build her confidence. Then she will be ready to go back to the world level and do great things.

It is the same in cricket. It's why competition, and the different levels of competition, are so important in the learning process. I recommend the following approach:

- use higher competition to facilitate higher learning;
- use same-level competition to gauge progress;
- use lower level competition to introduce new learning and ideas.

Moving forward

I've explained how, in batting, the intention should be to move forward towards the ball. Firstly, this puts the batter in a positive frame of mind, and secondly, it facilitates the correct unweighting into the active neutral position. The same attitude should be applied to your development. Always move forward; you can move back a notch if you need to. This leads to another golden rule:

> Always play at the highest level you can cope with and, when you're ready for it, push yourself forward to the next level.

This also applies to coaches and administrators when dealing with the development of their players.

The age group system

One of the problems with modern structured cricket is that we keep young players in age groups. A much better system would be to have young cricketers playing at the highest level of their ability. This would not be difficult to do. For example, instead of a group of schools organising their competition by age, they could organise it by ability, just as they do with their 'open' teams. Instead of the traditional system of the open teams, the firsts and the seconds, followed by the under-age teams of U16s, U15s, U14s and U13s, the under-age teams would simply be replaced by the thirds, fourths, fifths and sixths, etc. This way, all young cricketers would get to play at their correct level and be able to move forward.

I was playing senior cricket as a fourteen-year-old because I was ready for it. And it was very important to my development because I needed to test and push my whole nervous system. I had to cope with being nervous and anxious while at the same time concentrating on the ball, surviving, and making some runs at that level. Holding a player back in a lower level stunts their development.

Players and potential

Of course the problem also applies to elite cricket. The best modern example is Graham Hick, who grew up in Zimbabwe. Graham was a standout young player who had a burning ambition to play test cricket, but in those days Zimbabwe didn't play. So he decided to go to England to play county cricket and wait out the required time until he qualified to play for the English team. He had to wait seven years! So instead of playing test cricket at nineteen or twenty years old when he was ready for it, he didn't play for England until he was twenty-six. He had been playing in a competition for seven years that he was too good for, belting the ball all over the park and making huge scores. Consequently, he was never forced out of his comfort zone and his growth was severely stunted. He missed out on seven years of development because he was not stressed and stretched, and taken to the next level. When he eventually played for England he never achieved his potential. But if he had become a test cricketer at nineteen or twenty, I have no doubt he would have been even more successful at the test level.

We have had the same problem with young Australian cricketers. Martin Love, Darren Lehmann, Brad Hodge, Stuart MacGill and Michael Kasprowicz are all cricketers whose development has suffered by being held back. Your state of mind is different at twenty-eight to when you're nineteen. At nineteen you can do anything, you are very resilient. You might have a few setbacks, but you've had setbacks all your life so you are used to it. But when you are twenty-eight you know that you have limited opportunities and two or three failures could be the end. Darren Lehmann fits this scenario. He'd get a couple of games, then he'd be dropped, then a couple of years later he'd get another couple of games, then he'd be dropped. And the pressure that was building up on him was enormous.

The challenge

These top cricketers should be playing at the top level as soon as possible. Accept that they're going to have a few failures, but they'll learn from the experience. They need to be challenged. It's a problem which grows as cricket becomes more structured and increasingly career-oriented. The top guys stay around for longer. When I was playing we all retired in our early thirties, but now the guys play until their late thirties, so we need to devise ways of moving the talented players through. It's an important part of the selection process and a crucial strategy in cricket administration. If a fourteen-year-old is capable of playing in the Under 18s, that is where they should play. If a sixteen-year-old is capable of playing in an adult team, they should do so. And if they're eighteen and ready for first-class cricket, that's what they need to play — not Under 19s. Sachin Tendulkar played test cricket at sixteen. If you're good enough, you're old enough. Selectors ignore youth at their peril.

So a not-too-subtle change has occurred in the last twenty years and we have to adapt to make sure it works to develop our cricketers to their fullest potential. Right now, we need to be producing more guys like Adam Gilchrist, Matthew Hayden, Ricky Ponting, the Waugh brothers, Glenn McGrath and Shane Warne. I think it's a slight aberration that we've had such a good crop of players come through together to become one of the great sides of all time. That's not always going to be the case. The system of professional first-class cricket we've had in place for the last four years, England has had for forty years. Have a look at how many talented players, how many really expressive players they've produced in the last decade. Very few. We need to learn from their mistakes, not import them! We've got to encourage our young cricketers to move forward and provide a system that allows them to do it. The responsibility on selectors at the state level is to keep looking for young talent to push forward at every opportunity.

What can happen

I remember when our eldest son, Stephen, was playing junior cricket for West Brisbane and one of his teammates was waiting to go in to bat. He was batting at number four and was sitting in his chair with his pads and gloves on. He'd been waiting all week to bat and was very excited, but at the same time

I could see by his demeanor and constant fidgeting that he was very nervous and anxious. Before long someone got out, so he leapt out of his seat and ran to the wicket. It must have taken him fully thirty seconds! Because the batters had crossed he started off at the non-striker's end, and then the worst thing imaginable happened. The striker played the ball into the covers and called, 'Run!' It was suicide; our son's team-mate was run out virtually by the length of the pitch — gone first ball. Well, if it took him thirty seconds to get onto the ground, it took him thirty minutes to come off, dragging his bat behind him. He was crying, he was devastated. His parents were devastated too. In fact we were all devastated for him. The game was played over two Saturdays and he wasn't a bowler. So that was his cricket for the fortnight — one ball, run out. And I just looked at this kid that day and I thought, why would you play this game? It's so cruel. It's so final.

I don't want to return to the old days, but we have to change the structured approach so horror stories like this stop happening to our kids.

Learning by playing

In the real world you will fail three or four times for every time you succeed. Bradman succeeded one in two; other good players about one in three. But in today's structured environment kids are becoming so frightened, anxious and withdrawn, so scared of getting out, that it affects their free flow — they're frightened to play their shots and take chances with their bowling. You see, you've got to be allowed to fail. I learnt most of what I know from failing. Most of the good lessons I have got in life, but particularly in cricket, were that if I wanted to succeed I had to take risks, make mistakes, then correct them. I had to change either my approach or my technique or I would continue to fail. Our young cricketers do not get this crucial support from the structured system.

Today, when I look back, the unstructured and intuitive way in which we learnt the game was the perfect way. It doesn't matter whether it's the unstructured learning environment of the country that has bred so many great cricketers — from Bradman to McGrath to Gilchrist — or the fierce, combative backyard test matches that were such a feature of my city childhood. It trained our sub-conscious brains to play the game. It taught us a free and expressive style, how to handle stress and how to overcome problems, free from the horror of failure.

THE GOLDEN RULES OF LEARNING, TRAINING AND DEVELOPMENT

- Intuitive learning through a creative and unstructured environment produces exciting cricketers.

- Going to the cricket and watching it (free from commentators) teaches you about the flow and nuances of the game.

- Allow your imagination to take over — create your own cricket world.

- Feed your memory bank by playing and training in as many different environments and against as many different players as you can.

- Use 'targets' to develop your batting, bowling and fielding skills.

- Learn about stress through playing in a competitive environment (real or visualised) whenever possible — and make stress work for you.

- Practise and train the way you want to play.

- Wherever possible, simulate a match environment at training.

- Use specificity in your training.

- Batting is always a response (or reaction) to the ball that's been bowled (the stimulus).

- Batters must watch the ball. Intend to move towards the ball until you are forced back by the length.

- Power is achieved by the appropriate response to stimulus and the body parts working together to achieve the desired outcome.

- The primary concept of bowling is that it initiates and leads the play.

- The three fundamentals of bowling are consistency, strategy and an understanding that the batter's response is outside the bowler's control.

- In bowling, let the young body grow and become strong naturally over time.

- Use higher competition to facilitate higher learning. Use same level-competition to gauge progress. Use lower-level competition to introduce new learning and ideas.

- Always play at the highest level you can cope with and, when you're ready for it, push yourself forward to the next level.

- Don't try to teach cricket. It's too difficult to teach. Create an environment where cricketers can learn how to play the game.

CHAPTER 4

Organising Yourself for Success

Plan to succeed or prepare to fail.

In the introduction I mentioned that the top cricketers have very busy lives because not only do they play a lot of cricket, they are also busy organising themselves for success. This is the fourth of the five pathways to becoming successful in the modern game.

Organise yourself

In everything we do, we need to be organised. For something as simple as going to the beach we need to be organised. We need our sun cream, hat, towel and swimmers, we need some money, and we need to be clear on how to get there. Research says that understanding the direction we want go in aids motivation and priorities and, importantly, gives us feedback about our progress. If you have to be organised for something as simple as going to the beach, think about how organised you have to be to face bowlers like Anil Kumble and Shoaib Akhtar. And think about how organised you need to be to score a lot of runs against them.

Organising yourself for success is one of the most important skills that all the best cricketers possess. But what does it mean? It means organising yourself to:

- set goals and achieve them, step by step;
- have a positive attitude and be confident;
- concentrate effectively for long periods;
- be healthy;

- be fit;
- be aware of situations and tactics;
- reflect on your performance and ways of doing what you want to achieve; and
- develop as a person outside the game of cricket.

In chapter 3 I outlined the balanced cricket education I received during my childhood and youth. This was a combination of learning the basics from our coach, Lynn Fuller, and my father, and having plenty of unstructured play with my brothers and friends. It was an ideal learning environment.

Along with this learning, there were four other experiences that I look back on now as being crucial in my development.

School cricket

The first involves Chester Bennett, my cricket coach at school. Chester was an all-rounder who had played for South Australia and Western Australia and really enjoyed working with young cricketers. He was acutely aware that the difference between a *good* cricketer and a *very good* cricketer was what went on between the ears — I call it *programming the software*. Every Friday he organised a room for the team to gather around and talk through our cricket experiences. We'd use the time to explore why we played a certain shot at a particular point in the game, or why we used a particular bowler, or what the critical moment was during the innings for a player who made a hundred. This discussion allowed us all to think about our cricket and what had resulted from our actions. I realise now that Chester was aware of the importance of reflecting on your performance as a learning tool, and I can't recommend this sort of approach highly enough to players, coaches and administrators alike.

Loss of form

The second crucial learning experience occurred one day in Hobart when my brother Ian and I were playing in an Australian XI against the touring Rest of the World team. In those days Tasmania didn't play in the state competition so two or three mainland players would join a Tasmanian team to play a first-class match against the touring side. I'd started playing for Australia the year before, with mixed success. I'd scored a century in my first innings, but the next few innings were pretty ordinary, and I finished the series with a 60 against England in Sydney. I'd started off the current season in really good form, but

I was getting lots of twenties and thirties and getting myself out by hitting the ball in the air and taking unnecessary risks. I justified this by believing that I was trying to pick up the run rate — I was doing it for the team. The pattern continued against World XI in Hobart, where I'd scored about 20 in each innings and hit the ball really well.

One evening, towards the end of the game, I was waiting in the hotel foyer to go out to dinner with Ian and a couple of the World XI guys when the concierge came over to me. 'Mr Chappell, here's some mail for you,' he said, and he gave me a letter. I knew from the handwriting on the envelope that it was from my father, and inside was a newspaper cutting from the Adelaide *Advertiser*. The article was by Keith Butler, a long-time sports journalist, and the essence of the article was that I'd lost the plot as a test batter. Keith observed that my shot selection would cost me my place in the Australian team and ultimately the forthcoming tour of England; and that while I didn't look out of place in the Test environment, my inability to turn good starts into decent scores may limit my Test career. At the bottom of the article my father had added a handwritten note: 'While I don't agree with everything Keith has said, I do think there are areas of his comments you should think about.'

The word was out: I was doomed! You can imagine how I felt. I was pretty shattered — especially as in my own mind I was doing well, and I saw myself as a good team player too. But suddenly I wondered if Keith and my father were right. If so, I was letting down both my team and myself. The other guys arrived in the foyer, but by now I was in no mood to be sociable. I said, 'Look, I'm not hungry, I'm going to stay in.'

So I went up to my room and sat quietly in a chair. As the light faded over Hobart, I thought about what Keith and Dad had said, and about every game of cricket I'd ever played — the backyard, the beach, the park, school cricket, club cricket, state cricket and test cricket. Suddenly a light came on inside my head. Three things occurred to me:

- That when I did well I was thinking positively, and when I played badly I was thinking negatively.
- That ninety-nine times out of a hundred, in every one of those games of backyard cricket right through to test cricket, I had got myself out. Okay, sometimes good bowling had contributed to it, but a mental mistake on my part had cost me my wicket.

- And most importantly, no matter what I did for the rest of my career, ninety-nine times out of a hundred I would get myself out. It's what happens to everybody; it's inevitable.

So I decided that there were two things I had to do:

- I had to be *positive* (that old cliché of the power of positive thinking was crucial); and

- I had to *delay the inevitable dismissal*. And that the longer I could delay it the more runs I would make. One thing was certain, there was no chance of scoring runs back in the pavilion.

A positive routine

I realised, too, that there was a physical routine to it all. On those days when I performed well and was positive, I was in control of my environment. On the days I played badly other things controlled my environment. I was negative and allowed myself to be distracted by my thoughts:

> *This guy's a good bowler, I hope he doesn't get me out. I wonder what the selectors are thinking about me. I wonder what the crowd's thinking about me. I wonder what the opposition's thinking about me. I wonder what my own players are thinking about me.*

This kind of negative thinking harms your performance. It distracts you from focusing on what you are doing. I realised I had to focus on what I was there for — and that was to make big scores. So, in the darkness of my hotel room in Hobart, I committed myself to improving my batting. More than that, from that day on I committed myself to doing two basic things:

- I would formalise the concentration techniques that I had only used on an ad hoc basis to this point; and

- I would develop daily routines that would allow me to be positive and confident every time I walked out to bat.

I went to bed that night as excited as I've ever been because I believed I'd just discovered the meaning of life — and cricket *was* my life. And while I occasionally still made poor shot selections the incidence was vastly reduced. It was another step in the process of becoming a Test class batsman.

Loss of focus

A third important learning experience occurred in 1975. The year I started with the first World Cup, followed by a Test series in England. I was in good form at the start of the tour — very focused, with my routines in order. But just before the start of the series my wife Judy gave birth to our first son, Stephen. This was a huge moment in our lives and our relationship, and I found myself desperately wanting to be back in Australia. As history shows, I had a poor series, and when it ended I took some time to reflect on my performance. I realised that I had lost focus and strayed away from my routines, which I knew were critical to my previous success. This taught me an important lesson: It's no use trying to control things that are out of your control.

In trying to do this, I still wasn't able to help Judy and I'd also failed to do what I was being paid for. From that day on, I committed myself to focusing on the task at hand, knowing that I couldn't kid myself that I could satisfy two conflicting needs. For me, this was another important lesson in developing as a cricketer and as a person.

Routine

The fourth crucial experience occurred during 1981–82 when the powerful West Indies team toured Australia. I'd previously succeeded against this world-class combination of fast bowlers, and I was looking forward to adding to this success. By January 1982, I had just scored my seventh duck in a row, and the world didn't seem so rosy. I couldn't work it out. I seemed to be hitting the ball well enough in the nets, but I obviously wasn't getting enough time in the middle to confirm this. I remember walking from the ground a number of times, thinking, 'I didn't see that ball.' It was something I had never experienced in my whole career. I'd always prided myself on my ability to pick up the cues and the line of the ball early, and get into position.

On the final day of the Melbourne Test I was feeling pretty low, when the West Indian psychologist, Dr Rudi Webster, who later became the head of the West Indies Cricket Academy, came into our room. We started chatting about my situation and exploring potential reasons for my failures. As he later explained in his book *Winning Ways*, Rudi had identified the problem early on in the series, but for the obvious reasons of conflict of interest he'd waited until the end of the series to talk to me about it. Rudi was a shrewd coach, and he opened the discussion by getting me to talk about my feelings just after I lost my wicket. As the words came tumbling out of my mouth I knew that I had lost focus and wasn't following the ball as I had trained myself to do. Again, I had strayed away from my routines. Rudi didn't really have to say anything more. A net session the next day confirmed my suspicions and a month later I was in New Zealand making a hundred in the first one-day game in Auckland against the likes of Richard Hadlee, one of the best fast bowlers of the modern era! The solution was so simple, but moving away from my routine had produced such a huge consequence.

I believe these stories, drawn from my cricket career, serve as excellent examples for players and coaches of ways to initiate your thinking about organising yourself for success. Deciding what works for you, and having consistent routines that allow you to achieve your goals, are the keys to the really great sports champions such as Tiger Woods, Mohammed Ali and Sir Donald Bradman. I can't emphasise this highly enough.

I was asked to write this piece by the author John Marsden for his book *This I Believe 2* (Random House, Sydney, 2004). I think it gives a good precis of what I've been talking about so far in this chapter.

THIS I BELIEVE

The lessons I have learned from the team sports I have played have been invaluable to me in all aspects of my life. I grew up in a sporting family. Cricket, baseball and Australian football were our father's favourite sports so I was involved with all three from an early age.

Cricket was always going to be the main sport because Dad had a passion for the game. He soon inculcated that love to his three boys. Apart from playing the game, I watched, listened and read as much about the game and its heroes as I could. The big test matches of the era were those between Australia and England. I dreamed of one day representing Australia in an Ashes test series as I played my make-believe test matches in the backyard.

I did not actually believe I would be good enough to play for my country. As one of the smallest boys in each class in primary school, and for the first few years of secondary school, I always struggled to match it with the bigger boys. Even though I eventually grew to a height of 188 centimetres I still don't think of myself as tall because of that early experience.

The fact that I struggled because of my size, and a huge inferiority complex because of it, I had to develop other survival techniques. Because we usually played on cement pitches, which exaggerated the ball's bounce, I could not physically hit many balls. I had to learn to pick the balls I could and could not hit to score my runs. I also had to develop a few shots that the bigger boys did not need. It was a lesson in survival and creativity that proved invaluable later in my career.

Even as I grew and had success I could always identify other players who were much better than me. I was very nervous before games and sometimes found the pressure of waiting for my turn to bat almost overwhelming. Sometimes I almost wished myself out on reaching the wicket just to remove the 'sick feeling' in my stomach. I am sure I panicked myself into getting out on many occasions because of the pressure of wanting to do well to save personal embarrassment.

Despite all this self-sabotage I still managed to have some success along the way and steadily progressed through the grades. What I found was that the pressure increased rather than decreased as I made progress. As someone who had had some success before, there came an expectation, from others as well as myself, that I should keep scoring runs.

The lesson I learned through all this was that I got myself out more often than the opposition bowlers did. It was my mistake that usually led to my dismissal rather than good bowling. Often some good bowling contributed to my mistake, but in the end it was generally a mental error of mine that led to my dismissal.

One day it finally dawned on me that if I could take control of my state of mind I could change all of this. It didn't mean that I wasn't going to make mental errors but it did mean that I could delay the inevitable and bat for longer. I reckoned that if I batted for longer I must make more runs.

With that understanding I was able to relax and focus on the process of being successful rather than 'worry' about the outcome. My mantra became: 'Concentrate on the things you can influence and let the outcome take care of itself.'

Setting goals

*If I put a narrow plank on the ground and ask you to walk it, you won't have
any problem doing so. You would just take one step at a time till you reached the
end. But if I then place the same plank across two high roofs and ask you to
walk it you would have second thoughts because you would start to think of
what could go wrong and what might happen to you. Thoughts about falling
and injuring, or even killing yourself, immediately flash through your mind. Fear
and anxiety then sweep in as you become tense and tight. The task in both
cases is the same, but in one case you stay in the present and focus on the
process and in the other you go into the future and think about the awful things
that might happen to you. Goals motivate you to action but you must know
what action to take and how to take it.*

DR RUDI WEBSTER

We've all had those days that are aimless, where we just wander around from
one thing to another, not getting stuck into anything, never quite completing
anything. These sorts of days are fine once in a while to relax and wind down.
But if you want to achieve an aim or result, they are not the way to go.

How to set goals

To move forward we need goals (aims). They give us something to strive for,
something concrete to achieve at a certain point of time. Here's an example:

You're the all-rounder in the local cricket club. Last season you averaged 20
runs per innings and two wickets per match. If you could increase those scores
to 30 and three, you would not only be helping your club, you would go close
to getting selection in the representative district team. So you make that your
goal — a batting average of 30 and three wickets per game. Then, if the gods
smile down upon you, you could be chosen for the district team. Note that the
batting and bowling goals are under your control, whereas selection for the
representative team is outside your control. If your primary goal is selection
for the representative team, you may sabotage your chances of doing so by
focusing on the outcome rather than the process (batting and bowling well) of
what it will take to be chosen.

Goals are very important because without them you don't know where you're going. You have no real direction and operate on whim. You have no measure of success. Goals give you something to aim for; they give you a yardstick and feedback while you go along.

Without goals you can't plan, and as we discussed in chapter 3, planning is paramount for everything we do, especially in our preparation for cricket.

Goals help you improve. The all-rounder in the example created their own benchmark the previous season. Now they want to build on that performance and do better. But, as Dr Rudi Webster alluded to in the quote above, goals need to be taken a step at a time — you can't become a fighter pilot before you learn how to fly. So setting reasonable and attainable goals is very important. They should be neither too easy nor too hard; they should move you forward one or two steps in your development. And you need to be flexible enough to change them if necessary.

Plan for success
Once you've set your goals you need to plan how to get there — that is, you need to organise yourself for success. Here's where the various other components for success come in: a positive attitude, confidence, concentration, health, fitness, situational and tactical awareness, reflection and personal development. They are the components of your plan, and we deal with them in more detail later in the chapter.

John McGrath, a dynamic and hugely successful Sydney real estate agent, has a great goals system which he describes in his book *You Inc.* (HarperCollins, 2003). John recommends that you write down your goals (dreams, aims, whatever you want to call them) and first thing every morning when you get up, and last thing every evening as you go to bed, read them through so that you're continually reinforcing them. Every day, John commits to doing something concrete to reach those goals. Not something passive like dreaming about them, something concrete that takes him a little bit closer to achieving them. In fact, John plans his whole day around achieving his goals.

Take the first steps
Take a pen and paper now and write down your goals for this or the next season. Over the next few days think about them and fine-tune them, then write them out neatly or do a printout, and put it in a conspicuous place — by your bed,

on the fridge — or laminate it like John does and stick it up on the wall of the shower. Here's a template for you to follow.

Your goals need to be focused on the process of how you will achieve your desired outcome. A goal of 50 runs per innings will not be as useful as a goal to concentrate for every ball and play each ball on its merit.

A PLAN FOR SUCCESS

Everybody wants to have a successful season. Unless you have a plan it will be more good luck than good management if you succeed.

My goal for this coming season
You need to set a target for success for the season to help you keep focused and do the necessary work. It is important that you have an idea about what constitutes a successful season for you. For example, if you're a batter and you made 500 runs last season, you may set your goal at 700 this season; or for a bowler, 40 wickets last season and 50 wickets this season; or for a wicket-keeper 40 and 50 dismissals. Assess your previous benchmarks and take them a challenging step up from there.

Match by match
Figures such as 700 runs, 50 wickets and 50 dismissals can be pretty daunting, especially if you haven't achieved at that level before. Nobody can score 700 runs or take 50 wickets in one match so the targets need to be reduced to bite-sized chunks. Break your goals down into match goals. If the season consists of ten matches it is simple to break down your target. A batter will need to score 70 runs per game while the bowler will need five wickets and the keeper will need five dismissals.

Innings by innings
Break your goals down again. In ten matches it is likely that you will bat or bowl around seventeen times for the season. On this basis a batter will have to average around 40 runs per innings while a bowler or wicket-keeper will need around three dismissals.

Already the targets have become more accessible.

Day by day
As your season begins you can set separate goals for each day, which can be related to the conditions, the situation of the match and your overall season goals.

Session by session
It is important to have goals for each session. The clearer the goals are, the easier it will be to focus on the job at hand. The goals will vary depending on the match situation and the conditions. Always be flexible enough to change your goals if the situation changes. You may want to vary your goal upwards if you are doing well. If you are not

achieving your goals it may be wise to vary them down to make them more achievable. This may be important if your confidence is down.

Your team should also have session goals. For example, 100 runs in the session at around 3-4 runs per over, or three wickets at less than 3 runs per over. This will help you focus on what goals you need to achieve.

Over by over
Break down your session goals into goals per over and the process will start to seem much simpler.

Ball by ball
The final step is to break down your goals into each ball. Anyone can concentrate for one ball. That is all you have to do — concentrate for one ball at a time — over and over again! If you can learn to play your season one ball at a time, you are well on the way to success.

Play your season one ball at a time!

Setting goals and working out a plan to improve your performance are things that are completely under your control. You can design these strategies, you can organise them, and you can carry them out. Goals that can be easily measured against your plan are the most productive and motivating. With a good set of goals and a workable plan you'll find that the runs, wickets and dismissals will look after themselves.

Routines for confidence and a positive attitude

You can't expect to be mentally organised if you're not physically organised.

After the revelations I had in my hotel room in Hobart, I went to Melbourne where I was picked to play in the test match against the Rest of the World. This game became my first chance to try out my new plans. I knew intuitively that to be mentally organised I had to be physically organised, so I decided to begin my new routine from the moment I woke up in the morning. I wanted to get into a positive pattern right from the start of each day. I worked out how long it took to get ready — how long it took from the time I got out of bed to shower and shave, breakfast, clean my teeth, do my ablutions, get my gear ready and get out of the room. It took me one hour. I could have been ready in half the time but then I would be racing, and I found that if I was racing physically I'd be racing mentally. So I got ready in an orderly fashion, without rushing so my thinking was also orderly and sound.

Be organised

When we were away on tour we shared a room with a teammate. So, instead of sitting on my bed waiting for him to finish in the bathroom, I decided to take control of my situation — to be up first and in the bathroom first. I'd then get out of the room and have breakfast so my team-mate could use the bathroom and get himself organised. Then I'd come back and do my teeth and get my gear organised.

At home it was a little different because later, when we had kids, I had to allow for the inevitable disasters that happened around the place and things such as traffic hold-ups and car breakdowns on my way to the ground. So I had to allow myself a little leeway.

Think positive thoughts

Each day I made a conscious point of being aware of my thought processes. If I started to worry about things, or be negative, I would consciously stop myself, and start behaving and thinking positively. For example, if I started thinking things like, 'The Rest of the World team has some fantastic bowlers — I hope I make some runs,' I would consciously change my thoughts to, 'I'm looking forward to getting my next hit — I really want to get out there and watch the ball and try out this new thought process.' In other words, I consciously stopped worrying about the things I couldn't control and started thinking positively about the things I could control.

Walk tall

As my physical actions influenced my mental thought processes I started doing positive things. I walked positively, straight and tall. My body language had to be positive. When you're playing well you carry yourself differently from when you're not playing well, and I had to carry myself as though I was playing well.

I greeted people positively and with a smile, I spoke to them positively, and I started to realise that confidence was an emotion and that I could create it. Whether I made runs or not was irrelevant. If I believed I was in form, I'd be in form. But if I believed I was out of form, I would be out of form.

Confidence was the key to my new approach. Confidence is self-belief; I had to start believing in myself because if I wasn't going to, no one else was going to do it for me.

The good thing about confidence is that it's an emotional state, and for that reason it can be created out of nothing. If you think and act as though you are in form, you can create your own state of confidence no matter what your recent results may suggest.

Create a system that works for you

Once I'd got to the ground I had another system. I knew how long it took me to get organised and into the nets — to do all the preparation that needed to be done. So I had to arrive at the ground in plenty of time and in the right frame of mind. Then I methodically did all the steps that I needed to do to get myself right for the start of the game, including spending five minutes sitting quietly. Each ground and change room is different. At some grounds I would go outside; at other grounds I would find a corner somewhere. The aim was to get away on my own so that I could do a mental stocktake of where I was. I'd mentally tick off all the things I needed to do and fine-tune things that weren't quite right. Have you ever watched Formula 1 racing drivers prepare for a race? Because their sport is so fast and dangerous and there is so much riding on it, including their lives, they quietly and meticulously check through every detail and prepare themselves mentally for what's to come. It's the same at the elite level of any sport. All elite sportspeople physically organise themselves so that they can be mentally organised. Physical organisation comes first, mental organisation second, not the other way around.

Relax

The most difficult day of a match in terms of preparation is the first day, because you don't know whether your team is going to bat or bowl. Personally, being a batter, I would prepare myself to bat because I found it much easier to wind down from that preparation than to try to wind up after no preparation. But some days, things just don't go right, no matter what you do. You can usually tell the minute you wake up in the morning. Often you can turn it around and get back in the right rhythm by making a conscious effort. But there were some days I'd get to the ground and I'd be struggling and fighting myself to get back on track, and nothing I did would work; those negative grey clouds would just fill my head. I soon learned from experience there was nothing I could do — you can never win an argument with yourself. If you're battling with yourself — 'Come on, concentrate, you've really got to get yourself back on track here' — you'll never win the argument. You lose concentration because you're thinking about other things, and while you're arguing with yourself you can't physically watch the ball. So what I would say to myself in those situations was, 'Okay, it's going to be one of those days. Let's just relax and enjoy it. Let's just at least watch the ball. You know, if you're going to do something stupid at least give yourself a chance.'

Take control

Another attitude trap that cricketers fall into is underrating your opponent. It applies whether you're a batter, bowler, fielder, captain or coach. Say you're batting and a bowler with a second-rate reputation comes on to bowl. You think, 'This is going to be good, I'll get some runs here.' But it's a terrible state of mind to be in because you're now looking for the bad balls instead of just watching each ball and playing it on its merits. You're trying to *will* the bowler into bowling you bad balls, and I haven't yet learned how I can control someone else's thinking. It may be possible, but I've never been able to do it as far as bowlers are concerned. You can never win.

Even so, there'd be some days when the bowler would be running in and I'd just want to belt the ball into the middle of next week — usually it would be a spinner. And I'd be saying to myself, 'He's got to go.' It was batting suicide. So I would stop arguing with myself and simply give myself permission to be stupid. On some days I'd get out. I'd hole out with a lusty hit down the ground or jump wildly down the wicket and get stumped — and walk off thinking how stupid I was, *knowing* how stupid I was. But on other days I'd hit a couple of fours and say to myself, 'So, that was lucky. Is that better? Now let's get back on track and do it properly.' All cricketers do this, but the great cricketers change their attitude and take control of their mental processes. Steve Waugh is a good example. In the first part of his career he was prone to these rushes of blood, but in the latter part he showed superb mental control.

What I realised that night in Hobart is that I had to take control. If I was going to succeed at the elite level and if I was going to keep playing at that level, then I had to take control of my mental processes. I couldn't just leave it up to Lady Luck that I would turn up in the right frame of mind and that all the right processes were going to take place. So I started developing my new routines in the following match, the Boxing Day Test against the Rest of the World in Melbourne. Suddenly, I felt in control of my environment and success was immediate. I scored a century there and followed it up with another century in the New Year's Test in Sydney.

A routine for concentration

*Concentration is the platform on which
you build success.*

Mental techniques

Having played test cricket at a time when fast bowling dominated the bat, I was fortunate to have learnt early that concentration was the key to success.

In the second half of my career the West Indies had an awesome quartet of pace bowlers. The biggest thing to come to grips with when facing these bowlers was that it was going to take a long time to make runs. On average they bowled 12 overs per hour with a high percentage of short balls, often head high. If you faced half the balls bowled and half of those were difficult to score from you were effectively facing 3 overs per hour. This made it difficult to build up any momentum with your innings. Even with the best will in the world it was hard to force the pace and get on top of the attack. I decided that if I was going to score runs against them I had to be prepared to bat all day and not get distracted by the frustration of not being able to score quickly. To achieve this I had to develop my mental techniques to give support to my physical skills.

Using a routine

I had always prided myself on my ability to concentrate for long periods but I had to take it to a higher level during the period of World Series Cricket in the late 1970s. I learnt at this time that to develop a mental routine I had to have a strict physical routine. I developed a consistent routine between balls and between overs, similar to a golfer's pre-shot routine, in order to conserve my mental and emotional energy. This also provided me with checkpoints, so I knew I was concentrating before facing each ball.

My routine allowed me to switch in and out of the three different levels of concentration, which are explained in detail on pages 148–150. The first level, *awareness,* was the state of being aware of what was happening around me but not being acutely focused on any one thing. I used this while waiting to go in to bat, in between balls and in between overs.

I switched from *awareness* to *fine focus* when the bowler reached the top of his bowling mark. At this point I switched my focus to the bowler's face because it gave me an insight into his emotional state as well as his body language. I did this using my peripheral vision. From this I gained valuable information and cues from the bowler. As the bowler reached his delivery point I switched my focus to the point from which the ball would be delivered and I narrowed my visual field as I switched to *fierce focus.*

I used *fierce focus* for the shortest time possible because it required a lot of mental energy. As the ball left the bowler's hand, all I saw was the ball and the bowler's hand. This gave me all the cues I needed to gauge the line, length and type of delivery.

Conserving energy

Once that play was finished I looked to the crowd momentarily to give my mind a rest as I switched to the state of *awareness.* This was important to conserve mental energy. The cue to bring my mind back to the game was to count the fielders, then switch to the bowler's face as he reached his mark, and I cycled through to the state of *fine focus* on to *fierce focus* and back again.

I went through this process for every ball I faced. If I didn't, it was possible to get stuck at one level and either use too much energy too quickly or face balls without being properly focused. Each time I got back to the striker's end, having been away from strike, I re-marked my crease as a signal to my brain to begin the cycle once again. These physical actions triggered signals to my brain that it was time to start the process over again. They were also checkpoints for me to know that I was in the state of mind that would give me the best chance of success.

Results

Each time I went through a lean period in my career I was able to trace it back to the fact that I had got away from this routine. As soon as I got back to the routine my output of runs increased. I had learnt early in my career that ninety-nine times out of a hundred I would get myself out. The pressure built up by the bowlers may have contributed to it but it was a mental error that invariably brought about my dismissal.

I also realised that no matter how good my technique, this ratio would never change. I decided that I had to improve my mental skills so that I could delay the inevitable for as long as possible to give me a greater chance of making runs.

Concentration

Concentration is closely related to confidence and a positive attitude in that it requires routines for controlling your thought processes. That night in my hotel room in Hobart got me working on my concentration too. Leading up to the Melbourne Test against the Rest of the World, I decided to see if I could control and program my concentration in the nets. Even though there were three different bowlers coming at me one after another, I decided to treat each ball as a separate entity. I blocked out thoughts about the previous balls and the balls to come and concentrated solely on the ball I was facing. It felt good. I thought I could tell the difference immediately, so I decided try it out in the Test.

That's what concentration is: focusing on the things that are important at that moment.

I realised that prior to this time I was hitting the ball so well and enjoying it so much I was still basking in the glory of my previous shots as the next ball was being bowled. That's the same as playing and missing and continuing to worry about it after the event. If you've got that sort of stuff going on in your head while the bowler's running in to bowl you are setting yourself up to fail. I had to control my thought processes and actions — and my emotions too, because some days things didn't turn out the way I wanted.

So I started to develop a process of concentration personally tailored for me. I realised that I couldn't just turn up to the ground and stroll out to middle with a bat in my hand and start concentrating. It was a process that demanded time and build-up. That's why I started my routines from the moment I got up in the morning. In fact, I started preparing for the next innings immediately my last innings had finished.

The three levels

I worked out that there were three levels of concentration, like the gears in a motor car: neutral gear, first gear and overdrive. I called neutral the *awareness* level, first gear the *fine focus* level and overdrive the *fierce focus* level.

Awareness

In a car, neutral is where the engine's turned on and just ticking over. In my first level of concentration — awareness — you're aware of the situation and what's going on around you, but you're not really actively involved in it. You're a spectator, just observing; you're not using up much fuel (energy). That's your concentration level between games, when you're getting ready, waiting to go out to bat, waiting to come onto bowl, between overs, and even between balls. There are other things you can do in this neutral state too, such as observing the conditions and the opposing team. Is the wicket seaming or spinning; is it fast and bouncy or slow? If you are waiting to bat you could check out the fielders. Which ones are sharp, which ones are slow? How are they bowling? How are they batting? These are the sorts of things you can observe and soak up in neutral gear.

One of the dangers, and we've all done it as batters at all levels of the game, is to use up all of your mental energy concentrating for the batters before you. You're sitting on the edge of your seat hoping they don't get out because you don't want to go in just yet:

> *The ball's too new; the wicket's too green; they're bowling too fast; this guy's their best bowler and I really hope he's worn out before I go out to bat.*

If you've got all those thoughts going on while you're waiting to go in to bat, you're in trouble because you're using up a lot of the mental energy you'll need when you go out to bat yourself. And your energy tank is not a very big tank. I can remember playing games as a kid where I tried to concentrate the whole time. I'd get cramps in my arms and hands from gripping the bat so tightly, and concentrating so hard for so long. That's not the way to concentrate.

Fine focus

The second level — first gear in my car analogy — is *fine focus*. If you're waiting to bat and a wicket falls, or you've been called on to bowl, this is when you switch up a notch. You'll focus in on the conditions: 'The breeze is coming up, it will help my outswinger,' or 'The grass is long, it's going to be a slow outfield.' Then you slip back to neutral as you prepare.

So let's say I'm going out to bat. I've arrived at the wicket and take guard. This is the first message to my brain that things are getting serious. The next stage in my routine is to look around the field and, under my breath, count the fielders: 'Slips three, gully four, third man five, extra cover six, mid-on seven, mid-wicket eight and fine leg nine. Okay, here we go.'

Now I start concentrating on the bowler. I switch to fine focus. I zero in on the bowler's face. I need to know all about him; I have to get all the information that I need as he's running in to bowl. My peripheral vision takes in the rest of him, but his face tells me most of what I need to know. Bowlers give away a lot of information just by their facial expressions. I remember playing against the Pakistani spinner Abdul Qadir. Normally when he'd go back to his mark he'd flick the ball from one hand to the other, but when he bowled a wrong'un he'd have a little grin on his face. Obviously, as a kid, he'd had a lot of success with his wrong'uns and he used to look forward to it — he'd get excited and crack a smile! Richard Hadlee, Andy Roberts, all the bowlers that I played against, had little idiosyncrasies that gave me signals. Now, they weren't signals I could totally rely on, but they gave me a little bit of an edge over the bowler.

The bowler's body language also signals important messages. Are they relaxed or tense? If they're tense, they're probably not confident, so as a batter you can use that to get a psychological advantage. Others are bowling well and you know that they know it too, so in those cases you have to be especially careful. All these little things are important bits of information; they go into your subconscious, not your conscious thoughts, and are part of your concentration routine. One more thing: when you're facing a fast bowler you have a bit longer to go through the process, but when a spin bowler's on, the process is much shorter.

Fierce focus

So, counting the field was the first signpost; observing the bowler's face was the next. Now, as the bowler gets to their delivery stride, I switch into concentration overdrive — *fierce focus*. I flick my focus from the bowler's face to where the ball is going to come from at the point of delivery, and I zoom in so my entire field of vision is the ball in the bowler's hand.

This is the critical moment because it's at this point you need to pick up all the information to commit to your shot. If you wait until the ball is even a quarter way down the pitch, you won't have time. The ball and how it leaves the bowler's hand should give you all the information you need. Is it going to be short or full? Is it going to swing? Is it going to spin? Remember, you've experienced all this before in other matches and at practice. It's in your memory bank. And so you make the fierce-focus conscious decision to go and meet the ball. Suddenly you're on autopilot and the subconscious brain is organising all your movements. You don't think about it — it's automatic.

Then you drop back two gears, back to neutral, before starting the process over again.

Awareness — conserving energy

So most of your time is spent in *awareness* mode, a few seconds in *fine focus* mode, and barely a second in *fierce focus*. By concentrating in this way you use up very little energy. Once I had discovered this routine I never got tired when I was batting; I could bat all day and still be fresh. When you get mentally tired, you get physically tired. I never wore myself out mentally because I was only concentrating in small grabs.

I employed this method with a lot of success during the period we played the great West Indies teams, from 1975 through to 1984. The West Indies had the most fearsome and ferocious fast bowling quartet in the history of the game, yet my record got better and better. And that was only because of this system of concentration. You see, it took so long to make runs against the West Indies. Using four fast bowlers they only got through 70 overs a day instead of the normal 90. That's 12 overs per hour and so, on average, you would face six. Now half of those overs were short balls whistling around your ears which you couldn't play, so that cut your six overs to three — 18 balls per hour! There was no way you could make runs against them unless you had a method of being able to shut out all of the other emotions, the frustration of just not getting many balls, of not getting any momentum. So in a session you might make 15 runs — pathetically few. But you had three choices: you could say, 'It's too hard,' and give up; you could get frustrated and try to hit some fours and sixes and get out; or you could stay there, fight it out and make some runs. You just had to work on the theory that it didn't matter if it took ten hours to get 100. Without my system of concentration I could never have done it. I refused to let my thinking get ahead of itself; I refused to worry about what happened last ball; I refused to think about the next over or the next session. If you do worry about those things you can't achieve the *fierce focus* level; you can't get the critical close-up at the point of delivery that gives you all the information you need.

HOW TO CONCENTRATE

It is impossible to concentrate fiercely for a full session of play, let alone a full day's play. It's important to save your mental energy for the precise moment it is required. As discussed there are different levels of concentration and the sooner a player understands these and learns when and how to use these techniques, the sooner their cricket will reach full potential. The same principle and techniques apply when batting, bowling and fielding.

TYPICAL EXAMPLES FOR BATTING

Waiting to bat can be very difficult and will often have a profound effect on the success of an innings. It is important that you do not waste your mental energy in fine focus or fierce focus concentration — for example, concentrating on the innings of the batters before you. It will not help them and it will affect your chance of success. You need to find a way to remain alert and aware without using up too much energy. I found it helped to have someone to talk to while waiting. The content of the conversation was not important but by talking to someone else I was prevented from thinking too much about the situation of the game or letting negative thoughts come through. The great Australian all-rounder, Doug Walters preferred to play cards — not something I would recommend, but it worked for Doug.

Once at the crease your aim is to be able to move through the different levels of concentration as required. This takes practice and is as important to your success as practising your batting technique. The only place these techniques can be practised is at the nets and in simulated practice games. As I reached the crease I was still in the level of awareness. After taking guard I would switch to the fine focus level, focusing on the bowler's face. I remained fine-focused on the bowler's face until he hit the bowling crease. At this stage I switched to the fierce focus level, concentrating solely on the ball and the bowler's hand. This is when you pick up the relevant information on line, length, swing or spin to help decide what shot to play. Once the ball is dead it is important to switch focus back to the awareness level before starting the process all over again.

TYPICAL EXAMPLES FOR BOWLING

It's just as important for a bowler to learn to concentrate as it is for a batsman. Bowling takes as much mental energy as physical; once the mental energy is depleted it is difficult to bowl well. It is important to find the correct thought keys to aid easy movement into and out of the different concentration levels.

As you head back to your bowling mark you should be in the awareness level. At the top of your bowling mark, as you turn to run in, you should move into the fine focus level. By now you should have a clear idea of your line of attack and the individual plan for the facing batsman. Having a system of thought keys will help you to remain focused as you approach the wicket. As you hit the delivery stride is the time to move into fierce focus for the delivery and until the ball is dead. To conserve energy it is important to drop back into the awareness level until you reach the top of your run.

TYPICAL EXAMPLES FOR FIELDING

Fielding is very much like batting. Between balls is the time to relax in the awareness mode. When the bowler starts their run-in is the time you switch to the fine focus level. While the batter, wicket-keeper and slips fielder would focus on the bowler as they run in, other fielders should fine focus on the batter. The batter's feet are the first indication of line and length, so this should be your focus. The trigger for the fielder to change into fierce focus is when the batter moves into their shot. At this moment you switch your focus to the bat. Once the play is finished, the fielder should revert to the awareness level, until the bowler gets back to their mark and the process starts over again.

A NOTE ABOUT TRAINING

Training sessions need to be planned and organised to maximise the opportunity for both batters and bowlers to practise their concentration and mental techniques, as well as their physical skills. If practice sessions only work on the physical level a player's performance will plateau, leading to frustration for both player and coach.

Health

*For optimum performance you need good health, and good health depends
largely on what you eat and drink.*

Throughout my cricket career I was plagued by minor ailments including constant throat and sinus problems. This puzzled me at the time because it was
hard to understand why someone as young, fit and athletic as me could have
these continuing ailments. Later I found out why — my health problems were
caused by what I ate and drank.

Eating habits

Nutrition-wise, I grew up in a normal Australian family of the 1950s and
1960s. Meat was the basis of almost every meal, starting with bacon and eggs
in the morning, and we ate large quantities of fatty foods: steaks, casseroles,
sausages, chops and roasts. Stews and casseroles were one of my favourites
because they were quick to eat. And as far as I was concerned, the less time
spent at the table eating the better. Food was something I had to have to stay
alive, and for the most part I looked upon meals as a nuisance. Meals inter-
fered with playing sport, so when it came to a choice between skipping a
meal or missing out on a game of cricket, baseball or football, I always
skipped the meal.

If anything, my eating habits were worse after I began playing top-level cricket.
I rarely ate much breakfast, so by the time I arrived at the cricket ground in
the morning I felt hungry. There were always plates of sandwiches available in
the dressing room, and from as early as 10.00 a.m. I would start to fill up on
them. I used to 'graze' on them for the whole of the day (unless, of course, I
was out in the middle fielding), which caused my team-mates to wonder how
someone so long and lean managed to put away so much food. At lunch,
whether or not I was batting, fielding or just sitting in the dressing-room, I
would eat whatever was on the table — usually a heavy, meat-based meal which
would have been hard to digest. Cakes and biscuits followed at the tea break.

Every afternoon I would feel sluggish and it was most noticeable when I was
sitting in the dressing-room, waiting to bat or having batted. A feeling of

lethargy would come over me and sometimes I found myself nodding off to sleep. This would have been bad enough at any time, but it was a real worry if I was padded up waiting to bat. So I'd go to the back of the dressing-room and jump up and down to try to shake myself into a state of alertness. The problem was that it takes energy to digest food. Eat a heavy meal at lunchtime and you can count on feeling sluggish in the afternoon.

I didn't realise it at the time, but my diet as a cricketer was far from healthy. Most cricketers in those days had little or no understanding of nutrition. We tended to eat badly or hardly at all. This was especially true once the season got under way and we were on the road, travelling from state to state and staying in hotels. Knowing what I know now, I'm sure I would've been a better player if I'd eaten well. I would certainly have had more energy.

Then there was the milk problem. At primary school I was always one of the shortest and skinniest in the class. I was self-conscious about it and so I decided the best way to build myself up was to drink a lot of milk. In those days small bottles of milk were given out free at morning recess and I'd always go for an extra one if there were leftovers. On top of that I drank milkshakes whenever I could and at home devoured milk by the litre. My milk habit continued all through my teenage years even after I started playing first-class cricket.

By the middle of the season I would be feeling run down and would have developed throat and sinus problems of one kind or another. The standard response was to see a doctor and get a prescription for antibiotics. None of the doctors I saw seemed too interested in discovering the underlying cause of the problem. I wasn't too interested either. My one concern was to get rid of the sore throat, or whatever else was ailing me, so I could keep playing and not miss a game. In this way I gradually fell into an unfortunate cycle. Sore throats, doctors, antibiotics — they followed each other in an endless sequence every summer. On each occasion, the antibiotics the doctors gave me cleared up the problem. But the relief was never more than temporary. For most of the 1970s, the period when I was at my peak as a cricketer, I went from one sore throat to the next, from one course of antibiotics to the next.

It was a chiropractor, not a doctor, who eventually helped me break the cycle. I went to him for treatment for a neck problem, a legacy of an old baseball injury, which was causing me problems whenever I batted or fielded in slips for any length of time. The chiropractor asked me about my general health, and I told him about the sore throats and other complaints. He said he suspected there was some root cause and raised the possibility that my diet was to blame. I told him about the hotel meals, the fast food, the cheese sandwiches in the dressing room, the heavy lunches in the pavilion, and the milk. All this convinced him that my eating habits were the source of the problems. He gave me some literature on the pros and cons of eating red meat and consuming dairy products. It included a report on a recent comparative study of elite athletes in the United States, whose fitness had improved sharply when they gave up dairy products. There was also information about the allergic effects of dairy products, and about the health consequences of eating red meat. It was very general information, but when I read it I felt it had been written especially for me. The health problems described in it were *my* health problems. I was not entirely convinced, but I decided there and then to try abstaining from red meat and dairy products for the time being and see if I felt any better.

The experiment proved an immediate success. Within days my health improved. To some extent this may have been because I had conditioned myself mentally to feel better, but there was concrete evidence too. The post-nasal drip cleared — the one I'd had for so many years I'd stopped being conscious of it. My throat problems went away, and the new sense of well-being I experienced was extraordinary. I felt fitter and had more energy. For the first time in my cricket career I found myself actually enjoying the regular fitness training — running laps of the oval, and so on — which had always been a hard grind. I could feel the training doing me good instead of just making me tired.

That was in 1979. Since that day I have not knowingly touched milk, cheese or any other form of dairy product — and I've rarely eaten red meat.

Good nutrition and good health

The fact that I could feel so much better simply by changing my diet shows what huge influence nutrition has on our health and fitness. In fact, it's the first rule of good health — it cannot be over-emphasised and it cannot be repeated too many times. The state of your health depends largely on what you eat and drink.

I soon realised that good nutrition and good health were the keys to everything. I began to read everything I could get my hands on, and talked to everyone I could who knew anything about it. I experimented with different foods and gradually developed a plan for good health.

The key was to eat nutritious food. It meant not only eating more good food (vegetables, fruit and complex carbohydrates such as breads and pasta) but also less bad food. Generally, you need to cut your consumption of animal protein to a minimum. In fact, the closer you come to a vegetarian style of eating, the better your chance of achieving optimum health.

MY OPTIMAL HEALTH DIET

It is hard to be specific about what an ideal diet should consist of, given that each of us is different. But here is a recommended breakdown by proportions (weight, not volume) of the kinds of food we should eat each day to achieve optimum health.

Fresh fruit and vegetables	75%
Starchy foods (bread, potatoes, pumpkin, rice)	10%
Protein-rich foods (meat, fish, cheese, eggs, nuts, pulses, legumes)	7.5%
Sugar-rich foods (sugar, honey, dried fruits)	5%
Fat-rich foods (oil, margarine, butter, cream)	2.5%
	100%

This is the kind of breakdown that we should all aim for — both meat-eaters and vegetarians. Vegetarians would eliminate the animal foods, of course, but as a general rule the proportions for the different categories of food hold true. Fresh fruit and vegetables should comprise about three-quarters of your diet if you wish to eat as healthily as possible. This leads to a further question: what fruit and vegetables, specifically, should you eat and in which proportion? The short answer is: whatever's in season. Provided you eat a reasonable range you don't have to worry too much about which type. Variety and colour is the key. For instance, if apples and bananas are the only fruit you eat, then your range of fruit is deficient.

Balanced diet

People often talk about a balanced diet, but few people understand what the term really means. There is no doubt our health suffers when we have too much of some things or too little of others. Too much protein is bad, because protein tends to acidify the system, which in turn can result in a multitude of health problems — gout and kidney stones among the most common of them.

Too little fruit and vegetables are bad, because these are our main sources of vitamins, minerals and antioxidants. So, to me, a balanced diet is pretty simple:

> We should eat less animal protein and more fruit, vegetables and complex carbohydrates, all of which are rich in fibre.

Let me stress that this doesn't mean everyone should become a vegetarian. Not everyone is suited to the vegetarian style of eating, physically or emotionally. But there is no doubt that everyone could benefit by consuming less protein, especially if the protein has an animal source and therefore contains a lot of saturated fat and cholesterol.

Raw fruit and vegetables
The issue of the body's acid–alkali balance, known as the pH, is very important.

A Coffs Harbour nutrition consultant whose work I admire, Samantha Backman, points to the fact that raw fruit and vegetables are the only alkali-producing foods available to us. All other foods are acid producing — and animal protein is the most acid producing of all. The point she makes is that our bodies are best able to maintain a correct pH balance if 80 per cent of our diet consists of alkali-producing foods and 20 per cent acid-producing. In the modern Western diet, though, the proportions are the other way around — eighty per cent acid and twenty per cent alkali — which is the root cause of many health complaints, osteoporosis being just one of them.

There are other compelling reasons for eating raw fruit and vegetables. They are our best source of nutrients. Many nutrients are damaged or destroyed by the cooking process. Raw fruit and vegetables also provide the body with essential enzymes. Now I realise most people would find it hard to switch suddenly to a diet consisting mainly of raw fruit and vegetables, but it is nevertheless a goal to aim for.

Nutrition is not everything, but it is almost everything. There are things affecting our health that we cannot control: the quality of the air, the state of the weather, the danger of infection. However, there is one thing over which we have complete control: the food we put in our mouths. Where our health is concerned, this is the most important influence of all.

Fitness and Strength

*Fitness, to me, was about doing the least amount of physical activity
required to achieve the best result. Some of my team-mates called it laziness;
I called it efficiency.*

If you're going to play cricket to your best potential, or any activity for that matter (your work included), you need to be appropriately fit. As we've discussed, nutrition and good health are the first steps. But you also must condition the body to withstand long hours of concentrated physical exercise. You need to have good aerobic capacity and the appropriate muscular strength. For mental work and study, fitness allows you to concentrate better for longer; for physical work, fitness gives you the strength to keep going for sustained periods.

Fitness programs

Today there are a plethora of fitness programs that increasingly occupy the elite cricketer's time, and clubs and state associations have their specific programs. However, fitness to me was about doing the least amount of physical activity required to achieve the best result. Some of my team mates called it laziness; I called it efficiency.

Two popular forms of fitness training are long-distance running (jogging) and weights. I wasn't a fan of either — they made me tired and sore. If a captain, coach or fitness trainer said, 'Okay, we're going off on a long run today,' I immediately became disheartened because it wasn't what I wanted to do. If they'd said, 'Let's do a sprint session,' I'd have been fine, but a 10-kilometre run was not my idea of a good day out. I remember Don Bradman saying that he didn't need to do a lot of running because he got plenty when he was batting and fielding. He was probably right, but he also did a lot more batting than the rest of us.

Weight programs can be useful for strengthening certain muscle groups in the body under certain circumstances, but as far as heavy weight training is concerned, I'm very sceptical about its benefits for cricket.

Strength and conditioning

As discussed in chapter 3, I believe it's much better if you can apply the exercise directly to the game. This requires that you do strength and conditioning sessions as part of normal training sessions, following the exercise with the specific cricket action for which it was designed. This way the brain integrates the strength and conditioning session to the actual movement for which it was intended. If there's a significant time lag between the two, the benefits may not be as great.

Relating fitness to skills

When you analyse our game, everything we do is in short, sharp bursts — we sprint, rest and repeat. So it seems logical to me that we should do a lot of that sort of training. The more you can incorporate those types of exercises into your practice sessions the better. For example, running with pads on is very different from running without pads. These days, when I play an occasional game, the most tiring thing of all is running with the pads on. It's very different from the normal running motion because you have to run 'around' your pads. So, as a coach, I incorporate these sorts of training exercises into the practice session. When the players have had a bat in the nets, I then send them over to a 20-metre strip on another section of the ground where I get them to spend ten minutes running a series of ones, twos, threes and fours. It not only helps them with their aerobic fitness, but their batting skills too — and the fifteen minutes you usually get in the nets suddenly becomes twenty-five minutes of concentrated batting practice.

Do as much physical training as you can within your training session. Match the fitness training to cricket skills. Try not to double up: I'm a great believer in efficiency.

Fitness is an individual thing, and any fitness program needs to take into consideration individuals within the group. It's very important that coaches and fitness trainers are aware of, and understand, individual needs. For example, if there's a player who's 195 centimetres tall and weighs 100 kilograms, they shouldn't be doing the same program as someone who's 160 centimetres, 70 kilograms and built like a gymnast. The smaller person can do lots of running and bounding around, and they will be fine. But the big person shouldn't have to run up hills carrying big weights, for example; short, sharp sprint work is probably enough.

My program

Over my career, I gradually found the fitness program that worked well for me. It wasn't something that happened immediately, it developed slowly, almost intuitively, and was continually modified as my career matured.

In the mid-1970s when my eldest son Stephen was young, we bought him a backyard playground set that had a couple of swings, a trapeze bar and two rings. I remember being out in the yard with him one day, messing about, and I realised I could do some exercises on it as well. I hung on the bar and did some chin-ups and knee raises (hanging from the bar and lifting your knees to your chest). I'd read that knee raises were good for you, and doing them so that you raised your knees alternatively to the left side of your body, then straight up, and then to the right side, strengthened different muscle groups in the stomach. This is also a good stretch for the upper body. I'd also read that chin-ups — that is, lifting your own body weight — were good for you too. Chin-ups aren't as tiring as lifting free weights because there is a physical restraint on how many you can do: after a certain number the body just can't do any more. So it's hard to hurt yourself and hard to overtrain.

These were very simple exercises, but I actually found that they made me feel stronger. And they're so easy to set up and do. You only need a horizontal pole, suspended firmly about three metres off the ground so it can take your weight, and you've got your own gym!

Many years later I met a self-taught fitness and strength trainer whose name is Nigel Websdale. Nigel taught me a more sophisticated version of the chin-ups and knee raises than I'd developed through my own intuitive process, and it was a very good program. It operated on the basis of alternating your grip on the bar from what I call the 'underhand' grip for the chin-ups to an 'overhand' grip for pull-ups. Together with the left-side–right-side knee raises it worked to strengthen a very wide range of muscle groups. Nigel's program got my lower back and stomach muscle strength to the point where I could actually do full leg raises — that is, straight leg raises rather than the bent knee raises. It's a program that I believe works well for cricketers because it strengthens those core muscles which are so relevant to both batting and bowling *and* it's got its own in-built safety valve. Your body tells you when you can't physically do any more. This program made me as strong as I ever needed to be to play cricket.

NIGEL WEBSDALE'S FITNESS PROGRAM

Nigel Websdale is a fitness expert who has worked with sportspeople such as Pat Cash and Mike Whitney. When I decided to start on his program I expected him to tell me to go out and buy a bench and weights or some other state-of-the-art body-building gear. But all he wanted me to get was a length of one-inch galvanised iron pipe (water pipe).

Find an area around your home such as the backyard or garage where you can mount the pipe so you can use it as a bar. It should be about fingertip height when your arms are held aloft. Measure the length you need and note any fittings you will need to mount it firmly.

Please note: The pipe will need to be able to take your weight, so make sure you've chosen a spot where it can be mounted safely.

Purchase a piece of 30 millimetre galvanised iron pipe or similar, the right length to mount in your chosen spot. Don't forget the other fittings, bolts and screws you need to mount it.

It's that easy. Now here's the program.

CHIN-UPS AND PULL-UPS

The chin-ups I do are of the traditional type. I do them with an underhand grip on the bar; that is, with the palms of my hands facing me.

The pull-ups are virtually the same exercise, except that I have the palms facing the other way.

Between them, these two exercises ensure that all the muscles in the arms, chest and shoulders get a workout. Make sure you breathe out when you pull yourself up, then breathe in as you lower yourself. Full extension on lowering is critical. Don't cut it short.

These may be hard for you at first. If this is the case, stand on a chair and lower yourself down slowly. You will be amazed how quickly this develops your strength.

LEG LIFTS

Start these once you are confidently completing the chin-ups and pull-ups.

Hang from the bar with outstretched arms and repeatedly raise your knees to chest height. This exercise tones up the abdominal muscles as well as the lower back, thighs and buttocks. Do them slowly. Quality is better than quantity.

Raise your knees in three directions in turn.

1 Straight up so they are pointing directly ahead.

2 At an angle towards the left (towards mid-wicket).

3 At an angle towards the right (towards extra cover).

By raising your legs at angles, you exercise the muscles right across the abdomen. It's a good alternative to sit-ups and other abdominal exercises. Do not pull your knees up rapidly. You will derive the most benefit from this exercise if you raise and lower them slowly. As with the chin-ups and pull-ups, breath out as you raise your knees and breath in as you lower them. The reason you do this is to prevent pressure building up inside your body. If you breath in or hold your breath when you exert yourself, your blood pressure will rise and you will build up pressure in the lungs and abdomen. Breathing out releases the pressure and, importantly, trains the breathing patterns that are so critical in sports.

I rotate these exercises each day in a three-day cycle. There is good reason for this. Physiologists tell us that the process of toning our muscles occurs in two stages: (1) the muscle is broken down by overwork during the exercise itself; and (2) the muscle recovers and grows after the exercise. In other words, the improvement is actually achieved after the exercise is over. If you exercise the same set of muscles every day you will not derive as much benefit as you would from a three or four-day rotation. The muscles of even top endurance athletes go through a recovery phase after competing.

Gradually increase the exercises within your own limitations
If you haven't done any lifting for some time, you may well struggle to do more than one or two chin-ups or pull-ups to start with. It doesn't matter. Have a break, persist. Gradually build up over time within your own limitations. This program has one important advantage over weights: it is less likely to result in injuries to muscles and ligaments, for the simple reason that you never lift more than your body weight. If the strain becomes too great, you simply won't be able to pull yourself up. In other words, if you can't do it, you won't do it.

Sprint program

When Dennis Lillee returned to cricket from the back injury that nearly ended his career, he did some training exercises with a sprint coach whose name was Austin Robertson Snr. Austin Snr was an Australian sprint champion in the 1920s and his son, Austin Jnr, played Australian Rules Football for South Melbourne (now the Sydney Swans) where he kicked a hundred goals in one season. He was a very good footballer and became Dennis's manager.

Austin Snr gave Dennis a sprint program. When I saw what Dennis was doing I asked him about it and he gave me a copy of the program. For the last three seasons of my cricket career I followed that program — a lot of short repetition running. It was very good for my aerobic capacity, leg strength and general fitness.

The first phase of the program, which took four to six weeks, was running laps of the oval raising your knees as high as you could. Try this one and see how you go! The first time I tried it I lasted 20 metres! It takes some getting used to. So I'd do 20 metres, then walk for a while until I got my breath back, then do another 20 metres. Slowly, over a four to six week period, I built up my leg strength and aerobic fitness to a point where I could do a whole lap (about 400 metres).

But this was only stage one — to condition your legs to be able to do the sprint work. The next phase of the program was a series of sprints over three distances: 20, 35 and 50 metres. You would do five sprints over 25 metres at 25 per cent effort, five over 35 metres at 50 per cent effort, and five over 50 metres at 75 per cent effort. The next phase was to consolidate your fitness by jogging back to your start mark instead of walking. At each stage your fitness and strength was increasing, and over a twelve to fourteen week period you got to the point where, really, you could hardly have been fitter.

The other impressive aspect of the program — and this was very important for Dennis who was coming back from a debilitating back injury — was that it made you concentrate on the technique of running. It made sure that you used your arms and your knees properly — with your drive arm tracking forward and to the centre of your body, not across it. So it was an excellent program for posture, leg strength and aerobic fitness.

AUSTIN ROBERTSON SNR'S FITNESS PROGRAM FOR DENNIS LILLEE

Austin Robertson Snr was a former Australian sprint champion who worked with Dennis Lillee on improving his running technique. Interestingly, as Dennis's running action improved, so did his bowling action. To me, this is an example of how working on the macro issues in your game can have a positive effect on the micro issues.

I adapted the program for use in my own pre-season training. I used the program for the last three seasons I played and found it the most beneficial for my body type and the fitness requirements for cricket.

STAGE 1: 4–6 WEEKS

This first stage is to condition the legs and build up awareness that a strong arm action is critical to good running style.

The object of the exercise is to run 400 metres with high knee lift. To achieve the proper leg action it is necessary to drive the arms appropriately. I found that the first time I tried this I was only capable of keeping the high-knee running style going for about 20 metres and then I had to walk for a few minutes before continuing. It took me six weeks in that first year to be able to keep it up for 400 metres. After that it took me around four weeks.

STAGE 2: 4 WEEKS

This stage is designed to build on a solid level of fitness. The focus should be on quality running technique rather than speed.

5 x $\frac{1}{4}$ pace sprints over 25 metres;

5 x $\frac{1}{2}$ pace sprints over 35 metres;

5 x $\frac{3}{4}$ pace sprints over 50 metres.

(This is meant to be $\frac{3}{4}$ to full speed but not quite flat out. The focus should still be on quality action rather than full speed.)

After each sprint, walk back to the start and begin again without pause.

STAGE 3: 4 WEEKS

This stage is designed to consolidate an excellent level of fitness. The focus should still be on cementing a quality running technique.

5 x $\frac{1}{4}$ pace sprints over 25 metres;

5 x $\frac{1}{2}$ pace sprints over 35 metres;

5 x $\frac{3}{4}$ pace sprints over 50 metres.

(This is still meant to be a $\frac{3}{4}$ to full speed sprint but not quite flat out. Still focus on a quality running action.)

After each sprint, jog back to the start and begin again without pause.

At the end of this twelve to fourteen week program you should have a level of fitness that will fit you for any level of cricket.

I found that these two programs were all I needed to be aerobically fit and strong enough to play cricket at the elite level. I didn't need to run for miles. I didn't need to work-out with heavy weights in the gym. Instead, I found programs that suited my physique, my emotional state and the actual skills of cricket.

Situational and tactical awareness

*Ignore youth at your peril. Youthful exuberance is sometimes
better than experience. Experienced players sometimes know
enough to be cautious.*

It's not only captains and coaches who have to be aware of situations and tactics: it's every player in the team. If you're out on the ground and not emotionally involved in the game, you won't be able to contribute 100 per cent to the team, and you won't perform to your full potential.

Situational and tactical awareness is about being aware of your environment, being aware of what's going on around you, of what the players in your team are doing, of what the players in the opposition are doing. It's about being able to *read the signs*.

Captain

As a captain it's essential that you're able to read the signs because doing so leads directly to you understanding the flow of the game. If your side is batting, you will need to be asking yourself the following questions:

- Are we on top?
- If we are not on top, how do we gain the ascendancy?
- Where do we go from here?

If your side is fielding; you will need to ask yourself:

- Are we making progress?
- Are we controlling the game?
- If we are not controlling the game, how do we take back control?

As the captain of the fielding side, you will learn a lot from your bowlers' signs and their body language. They tell you whether they're tired, whether they're confident, whether they're frustrated and angry. This determines how you will react with them, whether you should encourage them or leave them alone, whether you should keep them on or give them a spell.

Bowler

The better bowlers I've played with and against, guys like Dennis Lillee, John Snow, Andy Roberts, Michael Holding and Joel Garner through to the modern day bowlers, manage their emotions extremely well. They still get frustrated, upset and angry, but they deal with these emotions, move on and perform. They compartmentalise their frustration or anger and by the time they're back at their bowling mark they're under control, thinking of the next ball. By contrast, a young bowler may not be as good at switching off, so they run in and bowl the next ball while still feeling angry, which has a bearing on how they bowl. It's important for both captain and team-mates to be aware of an individual player's ability to deal with their emotions.

Of course, batters need to be situationally and tactically aware too. As discussed in chapter 3, batting is a process of reacting, so the more you're aware of the opposition's tactics and the situation you're reacting to, the greater your advantage. All this information goes into your 'software' while it prepares for each ball.

Batter

As a batter, pick up the signals from the opposition. Identify the good and the weaker fielders. Note any outfielders with a weak throwing arm; there could be the chance of an extra run. Note any infielder who is slow off the mark; there could be a single in it. Alternatively, you might get fielders like Ricky Ponting or Jonty Rhodes who are very alert and exceedingly quick, so obviously you'd think twice before trying to steal a single from them. Fielders and the quality of the fielding affect how you run between wickets. Who your batting partner is also affects your running between wickets — their style and abilities alter your judgement about whether you'll be bold or cautious. For example, they might be a bit slow or super quick. You need to be aware of these things to achieve maximum benefit for the team.

RUNNING BETWEEN WICKETS

Both batters call every ball — be aware of body language
Running between wickets is a critical part of building partnerships. A team that runs well together can put a lot of pressure on the opposition. Good running is based on good communication and good communication must be a two-way process.

I have always believed in the adage that two heads are better than one. That lesson was learnt the hard way when I was run out on a couple of occasions early in my cricket career. On both occasions I relied on my partner's call and on both occasions his judgement was found to be faulty. My father discussed the situation with me and between us we decided it was important for both partners to call, and that I should take a greater role in preserving my own wicket rather than rely solely on someone else's judgement.

From that day on I called every ball that was bowled and I called loud and clear. There were three calls — 'Yes', 'No' and 'Wait' — and I used one of them for every ball bowled. It was amazing how many more runs I made once I took control of my own destiny and how much more positive my partners and I became once we gained confidence in each other's judgement.

I have a few key rules in calling:

1 The calls should be loud, clear and early.

2 A negative call from either partner means you go back to where you started from as quickly as possible.

3 If you hit the ball well you should call 'Wait' because if a fielder gets to the ball it will have got to him so quickly that the chance of a run-out is high.

Situational and tactical awareness is also about communication. Let's look at the batting partner scenario again. When running between wickets, as you cross, tell your partner how you're going. You might be running towards the end where the ball is and they are running away from it. Be aware of the overall situation. As you cross you can say 'one', 'two' or 'three' to let your partner know what you're thinking. Then you can both run accordingly. As you pass on the second run ask, 'How are we going?' And your partner can reply, 'Yes, it's three,' or 'No, it's only two.' You need to keep communicating so you both know what the other's thinking.

Some of the better running partners have got so used to each other that they only have to look at each other to know that they are ready to run. Facial expressions and body language are some other forms of communication, but I always relied on vocal communication at the start and during runs.

Fielder

I remember Doug Walters and I often used to field alongside each other. We would make a pact, a challenge that nothing would get between us. It would make us more alert and gave us that extra reason to be on our toes.

Doug was an expert at situational and tactical awareness. In the field he used to love trying to trick the opposition batters into taking a single when it wasn't on. He'd sneak back a little from his fielding position and I can remember my brother Ian, who was captain, looking up and gesturing to him, 'Come in!' And Doug would have his hand behind his back, waving it like a tail from his bum — the sign for 'I'm just foxing'. So Ian would say, 'Okay,' realising that Doug was under control and knew what he was doing. Of course, not all fielders are as experienced or foxy as Doug; some go to sleep on the job, so the captain has to be aware of the strengths and weaknesses of each team member.

Team player

The list of things you can do as an individual team member to be situationally and tactically aware is endless. But here are a few recollections from my playing days.

- When you're in the field and the opposing batter is on 49 or 99 you know that in most cases they will try and push a single. So what do you do? Talk to the fielder alongside you, and together put extra pressure on the batter by trying to cut off the single. Force them to hit a boundary to get their 50 or 100. What's actually happening here is that you're working with the bowler to help get the batter out because you're helping put the pressure on. Whereas, if you're sound asleep, hanging back in the covers, and the batter drops one at his feet and gets the single, you've let the team down. Alternatively, if a batter's on 96 they might try to hit a four. In this instance you may drop back a little. You can assess the mood of the batter, how they're playing, to help you make your decision.

- Some batters play and miss a lot, whereas some batters often nick the ball. So if you're in the slips, take this into account. I remember fielding in the slips during the 1974–75 series against England with Dennis Lillee and Jeff Thomson bowling. You just *knew* Dennis Amiss was going to nick one. Keith Fletcher was always going to nick one. So you were a little bit more alert when those two were batting because you were tactically aware of what was going on. Some batters are strong on the leg side, like V. V. S. Laxman. If I was fielding at mid-wicket for V. V. S. I'd tend to move a little squarer.

- If you've got some tactical or situational information that you think is useful, tell the captain. Ask them, 'Do you want me to field a bit squarer for this player?' The captain might reply, 'That's a good idea,' or 'No, we're going to be attacking just outside off stump and if there's a gap it might increase our chances of getting them out, caught in the slips.' So, you don't want to override the captain because they might have it worked out, but it doesn't hurt to check.

Reflect on *your* last game and come up with some situations where you could have been more tactically and situationally aware.

Reflection

I owe as much of my success to periods of reflection as to training.

I discussed at the beginning of this chapter how my cricket coach at school, Chester Bennett, would hold a team meeting on Fridays where we would reflect on our performances both individually and as a team. Reflecting on your performance is very important because it raises issues that otherwise you may not consider. Take, for example, my form before the Melbourne Test against the Rest of the World: I was blissfully unaware there was a problem. Had it not been for my father sending Keith Butler's article, and my own ability to reflect, I would have just gone blindly on. Instead, I discovered routines and techniques for developing confidence, a positive attitude and concentration that I continued to use for the rest of my career. These had a huge influence on my overall success — they still do. Similarly, reflecting with Dr Rudi Webster on my game after that horror run of seven ducks in a row against the West Indies enabled me to go from a string of failures to a string of successes.

In other cultures the importance of reflection is well understood. The Japanese use the same word for 'reflection' as they do for 'practice'. They see the two as synonymous. Research indicates that learning may continue up to several hours after the activity, when the mind has had time to process the training and reflect. Allowing ourselves time to relax and reflect on what we have learnt is often more valuable than doing extra practice and trying harder.

Stop and think

There are two great things about reflection: you can do it anywhere and at any time. All you need to do is stop and think. How easy is that? You can reflect on things any time, day or night. You can even be reflecting when you're batting, bowling and fielding — during your concentration downtime. As we discussed earlier, if you are concentrating properly there are low-level concentration periods between balls and overs. Reflect on what's happened so far in your innings or bowling spell. At the end of your innings, spell or session in the field, reflect on what's happened. Ask yourself some questions: 'What worked and what didn't? Is the way I'm thinking right now helping the way I bat or bowl or field? Is there something I can do differently to help me bat or bowl or field better?'

Reflection is closely related to the things you think about in situational and tactical awareness. You can reflect on whether you're doing enough in the field to help the team take wickets: 'What else can I do? Do I need to concentrate better? Do I need to be fitter? Do I need to be stronger?' It's the same with your batting and bowling. When I prepared for the next game I would reflect on what happened in the previous game to see if there were lessons to be learned. And I would reflect on what I'd been doing in my training to make sure I was dealing with those lessons. It's a good idea to reflect on your training sessions in advance, too, to make sure you get the most out of them. Then, at the end, you can ask yourself, 'Okay, did I get all I could have out of that session today, or was there more I could have done?' And you can tick things off to make sure you're moving forward. You should be continually planning, checking on yourself, editing what you're thinking, editing what you're saying, editing what you're doing, to make sure you can do it better next time.

Do you see now why reflection, goal-setting, planning and situational awareness are so important and how they are so closely linked? Put simply, reflection is the adjustment phase of your goals and plans. Even when I was a kid, those nights after I had played all day in the backyard, at the park or on the beach, I would be thinking, even without knowing it, about what happened during the day and how I could do it better next time. That's reflection. It's continually checking on your growth as a player and as a person to make sure that you can do it better. That's really all reflection is: no more, no less.

Personal development

Human beings are learning beings — we're here to learn and grow. I'm a committed lifetime learner — that's a major part of my journey. I also value my spiritual development. Not in a religious sense so much, but simply developing love, compassion and care for my fellow human beings.
JOHN McGRATH, *YOU INC.*

When I took control of my cricket life, it helped with my off-field life as well. And when I developed interests and passions off the field, these, in return, helped my cricket.

I was lucky during my early career in South Australia. During the winters I had the opportunity to play two seasons of County Cricket in England, but I realised part way through the second season that full-time cricket was not what I wanted to do with my life. I wanted to capitalise on my cricket talent, but I found playing seven days a week pretty boring and I was getting into bad mental habits. I wanted a career outside cricket. So I wrote to my father back in Adelaide and I asked him if he could source a job for me for when I got home.

In County Cricket there is a lot of downtime, so I started buying books. They were mainly biographies and autobiographies by and about people whose lives had been successful. They were sporting people, business people, real estate people, insurance salespeople, politicians, and all sorts of people, usually self-made. And I found that no matter what endeavour it was, there was a common message in all the stories — that a successful result depended on a process. In other words, these were stories about people with *success skills*.

It was reading these books that gave me the understanding to be able to reflect the way I did that night in my hotel room in Hobart. In a way, that night was the culmination of my reading.

So I told Dad the careers that I was interested in — mainly sales and marketing — and it turned out that Mum played tennis with the wife of a sales manager at the AMP Society. Through that connection I got to meet the people at AMP and joined the company as an insurance salesman. I was twenty-one. AMP put me through training courses and sent me to seminars where the trainers talked about success skills, positive attitudes and confidence — all things that were relevant to my cricket.

A few years later I joined Coca-Cola Bottlers. The South Australian franchise of Coca-Cola Bottlers was one of the most successful bottling operations for Coke worldwide. Coke put me through a management traineeship where I spent six months in each department. I was sent to lectures, conferences and personal growth seminars where I learned more about positive attitudes, confidence, self-esteem — in other words, success. It was fantastic. They introduced me to Dale Carnegie's famous book on the power of positive thinking, *How to Win Friends and Influence People*, as well as *Psycho Cybernetics* by Maxwell Maltz, about boosting confidence and self-esteem — I found it fascinating to learn how the brain worked in this area.

Later, I moved to Brisbane to captain the Queensland state team, and what I had learned at AMP and Coke helped me significantly in my leadership role. I also set up an insurance agency and continued my quest for knowledge and personal development. It's crucial that, as a cricketer, you look outside the cricket arena and develop other interests and passions. These days, the Internet makes finding information so easy: you can look up material on any topic by experts from all over the world. You can find out about nutrition and fitness, and how the body and the brain work. You can find out about the power of the mind and positive thinking. You can even do a degree!

Empower yourself

What sorts of things can you do to improve yourself? Here are some suggestions based on things I've done.

- Probably the most important is to develop a positive mental attitude.
  Read books, listen to tapes, go to the movies, be a 'doer', mix with

positive people. Don't mix with people who are negative or pull you down.

- Find out all you can about nutrition, health and fitness — what's best for you.

- Life is about continuing to learn and grow. If you're no longer at school or university it doesn't mean you stop learning. Develop interests outside cricket: go to personal development seminars and expos, join a mentor program, join interest groups, read books, do courses, take a degree.

- Observe what successful people do. Read about people who have made a positive impact — you'll see that most of them are positive and happy, and all of them are doers. Learn from their achievements and mistakes.

So personal development is really about continuing to learn — about wanting to learn more.

TEN GREAT BOOKS FOR PERSONAL DEVELOPMENT

How to Win Friends and Influence People, Dale Carnegie

Creative Visualisation, Shakti Gawain

A Revolutionary Way of Thinking, Dr Charles Krebs and Jenny Brown

The Inner Game of Golf, Timothy Gallwey

Think and Grow Rich, Napoleon Hill

Psycho Cybernetics, Maxwell Maltz

The Seven Spiritual Laws of Success, Deepak Chopra

Supertraining, Dr Mel C. Siff

Rich Dad, Poor Dad, Robert Kiyosaki with Sharon Lechter

Winning Ways of Past Champions, Dr Rudi Webster

If these books are not available through your local bookshop try www.amazon.com and www.chappellway.com.

Failure can be the road to success

You'll find that successful people make lots of mistakes and have plenty of failures. Probably the most famous example is Thomas Edison who tried 1231
times before making an electric light bulb that worked. Someone asked him
what it was like to have failed so many times and he said, 'I didn't fail, I found
1231 ways not to make electric light.' Not only was he positive, he persevered!
Richard Branson, of Virgin fame, has tried hundreds of different things and
found two or three that worked really well. He's had a lot of failures, but it hasn't
stopped him. Unfortunately, most people fail once and think, 'Oh, I'm not
going to do that again,' and stop trying. They give up.

There's a great saying: 'You haven't failed until you've stopped trying.'

All the successful people I know have failed. Some of them have been broke
two or three times and have fought back. We learn to walk by failing. We get
up and we fall down, we get up and we fall down, until we finally work out how
to walk. Even Don Bradman failed 64 per cent of the time. He batted eighty
times in test cricket, yet he only scored twenty-nine hundreds. I survived in test
cricket by working out that I made a hundred every five or six times I batted,
so each failure was one step closer to my next hundred. And I learnt to think
this way from observing and reading about successful people.

Learn about success

No matter what walk of life they're in, successful people have worked out a system. They have a process they adhere to and they persevere. This is the most
important success formula I know. And you either learn it from your own experience or from other people. If you don't like reading books, try audio tapes or
videos, use the Internet, go to seminars or talk to experts. By whatever method,
learn the *traits of success*.

Keep it simple

The hardest thing I've ever done is parenting. What do you do when you're
confronted by those problems you've never dealt with before? There was no
manual, so I called on all the experiences of my life, particularly the things I'd
learned in cricket because that's where most of my life experiences had been.
I always tried to simplify the problem and deal with it in the simplest way,
because the more complicated things are the less likely that they are to work.
So, having learned in cricket to 'keep it simple', I applied that to bringing up

my children. In fact, I've applied that philosophy throughout my life to whatever I do. I think it was my mother who originally showed me that.

Prioritise

Successful people prioritise well. If they have a number of problems they prioritise them and deal with the most important one first. If you work this way it's amazing how the other problems become less significant; they fade away. However, if you start with the insignificant problems you never get around to the big one. The beauty with sport is that it forces you to deal with the big ones first. It forces you to keep getting better otherwise you'll fail — either as an individual or as a team. And the beauty of sport is the immediate feedback. The scoreboard always tells you how you're going.

One of the best books I've ever read is *Think and Grow Rich* by Napoleon Hill. It was a series of interviews with successful people. It didn't offer a recipe for success, but reading between the lines you could glean it from what these people had done. What they did was simple: they thought about what they had to do, they prepared a plan, and then put it into practice. They worked out the steps they needed to put into place to be successful and they did it. It's as simple and as difficult as that.

There's no doubt that my career and personal development outside cricket helped me develop as a cricketer. Equally, cricket helped me in my outside career and personal life. It cut both ways. The better you are as a person, the more growth you achieve, and the better you're going to be in all walks of life.

Organising yourself for success is a journey of self-discovery — of developing a positive attitude, confidence, skills, concentration and endurance, health and fitness, tactical awareness and an ability to reflect and to develop as a person. It all adds up to being a better cricketer.

*If you meet someone who's never failed, you've met someone
who's never tried.*

CHAPTER 5
Leadership

Every member of the team must realise they have
a leadership role to play.

In the introduction I mentioned briefly how leadership is not just the domain of the captain, vice-captain, coach and administrator. Every member of the team has a leadership role to play. Strike bowlers and top-order batters have a leadership role. Every fielder has a leadership role: to help the bowlers put pressure on the opposition batters and help get them out. Tail-end batters and part-time bowlers have a leadership role to play too. In the case of the tail-enders it's to round off the innings and make sure the team scores a sizeable total. If there has been a collapse, their job is to consolidate the innings; if it's already a good total, to make it even better. In the case of part-time bowlers, their job is to support the main strike bowlers by adding variation into the attack, making the big breakthrough, and keeping pressure on the opposition team.

Although the common notion of leadership revolves around a person in charge who gives orders, leadership is much more complex than that. Leadership starts with you. It's about getting yourself organised to run your life well, to take responsibility for yourself and your actions, and to make a difference to those around you. My old friend Paul Sheahan, who played with me in the Australian team, is now headmaster of Melbourne Grammar School and an acknowledged leader in the broader Melbourne community. He sees leadership for his students as:

> *Related to the capacity for people to have ideas, to articulate ideas, to evaluate them and follow through. Leadership is found in people who have a combination of qualities which encourage others to grow. But you don't have to become one of the captains of industry! It begins with being confident about the self, to determine what's best for yourself in the context of society.*

You can see from the points Paul and I have made that leadership is very much about teamwork, and teamwork is crucial to a successful team. Make a commitment right now to become a leader in your team.

THE 'TEAM BEFORE ME' ATTITUDE

TEAM SPIRIT

The five 'hows' of team spirit — your attitude towards each other on the field — are:

- how you respond to each other;
- how you help the other team members who are in difficult situations;
- how you combine indivdual thought-processes and skills;
- how you cover weaknesses and promote strengths;
- how the individual team members come together when the pressure is really on.

It's easy to have a good time off the field. What counts is having a good time on the field, which flows from a good team spirit and team achievement.

TRANSPOSE TEAM ENDEAVOUR INTO A PLAN

BATTING

The objective is to score as quickly as the situation and conditions allow.

- As a group we need to aim for 60 singles per innings. Achieve this by setting smaller targets: 20 per session, 10 per hour.
- Batters need to work in teams. Help the new batter get off the mark, look to rotate the strike whenever possible, take a 'one day' attitude to running between the wickets.
- Create partnerships, and once a pair starts to build something, work towards incremental targets. If we have 1 x 50, 1 x 75 and 1 x 100 run partnerships statistics show that we will make 300 every time we bat.

BOWLING

The objective is to take 10 wickets as quickly and as cost-effectively as possible.

- Maidens — Tailor your over to the batter. Ensure that you start the over well and work at concentrating for every ball. Aim to bowl maidens, therefore building pressure on the scoreboard as well as mentally over the batters.
- Team maidens — Consecutive maidens count as one team maiden. Be aware of what is happening at the other end, and if your bowling partner bowls a maiden, aim to get a 'team maiden' up for the group.
- First and sixth ball — Aim to bowl 'dot' balls at the beginning and end of each over to create and maintain pressure.

FIELDING

The objective is to do everything possible to assist the bowlers to take 10 wickets as quickly and as cost effectively as possible.

- Be positive in your physical presence (body language) and mental outlook (vocal and team-oriented actions) at all times. Be personally responsible for controlling your area on the field. Help out a 'partner', and keep focused and enthusiastic about their role in the fielding team.
- Be aware of what the bowlers are trying to achieve and field with determination to help them achieve their goals. Help create that maiden.
- Create six saves per day that help the bowlers in their role.
- Don't forget the one percenters. Involve yourself in as many 'plays' as possible. Always back up throws, cover other fielders' backs, get to the bowler's stumps, and make every throw perfect to the keeper.
- If done consistently all these little things add up to create an imposing package.

Captaincy

Leaders are inclusive at all levels.

While a sense of leadership is important for everyone in a cricket team, including coaches, administrators and others, the key leadership role belongs to the captain. This is simply because it's the captain who has to make those split-second decisions under pressure out on the ground that can change the course of a match. It can't be the coach and it can't be the administrators because they're not part of the action. The responsibility for running the direction of the game falls to the captain. This is the way it has always been, and in my view should continue.

State level

Only after I had played four seasons of first-class cricket for South Australia, a couple with Somerset and my first two or three series of test cricket did I ever think of captaining Australia. By that stage my brother Ian was captain of the national team, and of South Australia.

I had realised all those years before, playing in the backyard, at the park and on the beach, that there was a lot more to cricket than batting, bowling and fielding. And now I wanted the challenge and responsibility of making the ultimate decisions on the field. I knew, however, that if I wanted to captain Australia I had to have some experience at the first-class level and, fortunately, I was offered the captaincy of the Queensland state team.

It turned out to be much more complex than I'd ever imagined. There was a lot more involved than deciding whether to bat or bowl if I won the toss, or who batted where, and when to change the bowling. Captaincy required an understanding that each individual's mental processes had as much to do with their performance as their physical abilities. Each player had to be treated as an individual. This way you could work with them to maximise their performance for the team. Captaincy also required that you had an understanding of the history of the game and that cricket, the sport, was much more important than any individual or team. At times maintaining such a perspective was difficult. There were considerations such as playing entertaining cricket even though your team was struggling; and understanding that the media had a big influence on how players, teams and the game were perceived by the public.

National level

Of course, the ultimate accolade is to be asked to captain your country and when I was given that honour I accepted it in the knowledge that the 'legacy' of Australian cricket had been passed on to me and my generation. It was not a responsibility that I took lightly and there were times when it weighed heavily on my mind. But all the Australian captain can hope to do is to cherish that legacy, make decisions with the best intentions possible for all concerned, and pass it on to the next generation for safe-keeping.

For the first hundred years of cricket the Australian captain set the direction for the team's style and approach. He was the tactician and decision maker during the five days of a test. On tour he also had to be a selector, organise practice, work with certain players on their game and give speeches at various events and occasions. At home there was less to do as the players would join the national team from their home state teams, have one or two practices and then go straight into the test match.

With the advent of the one-day game and World Series Cricket in 1977, and the growing demands of the modern media, captaincy took on a whole new meaning. Not only was the captain the leader, tactician and in my case batter and bowler; he also became the marketer, administrator and media manager. The demands on the captain to become the 'face' of the team for the press and to involve himself in setting up the modern game were huge. I remember coming off the ground after a day in the field only to go into a lengthy press conference followed by management and strategy meetings on the development of the game. It became exhausting.

Vice-captain support

I relied heavily on my vice-captain, Rod Marsh. Rod was a great sounding board and a great conscience. I know he was fantastic support for my brother Ian when he was captain and he certainly was for me as well. He was very direct: there was no nonsense with Rod. He would keep you on the job, keep you very honest. For example he would say, 'Come on, it's time for a bowling change.' And I might say, 'No, I want to keep him on for another couple of overs. I've got a feeling he'll break through.' 'Nah, you're kidding yourself,' Rod would say. Some days we would disagree and some days we would agree, 'Okay, you're right. We'll take him off.' Rod played a key leadership role in the team.

I'd often delegate things to Rod: 'Keep an eye on the field for us, watch the angles, make sure the blokes are in the right place.' I remember in the Centenary Test against England I was bowling a long spell in the afternoon session on the last day and fielding in the slips between overs. The pressure was on and it looked like we would be defeated. England was going well, with plenty of wickets in hand. Derek Randall and Dennis Amiss were batting and all England had to do was bat out the day and they were sure to win.

I decided that our best tactic was to dry up the runs so that time became an issue. This way they would be back under pressure rather than knowing that all they had to do was keep batting to win the game. I hoped that with the pressure on them instead of us they'd make some mistakes and we'd get back in the game. I figured our best approach for a defensive attack was to have Dennis Lillee and the other fast bowlers operating at one end while I bowled a spell of medium pacers at the other. So we'd tighten it up and if we got a wicket or two the pressure would start to build.

After six or seven overs I was starting to feel the pressure myself. I hadn't done a lot of bowling that season, so I was out of breath at the end of my overs. With the demands of captaincy and the continued concentration required in the slips, I was becoming mentally drained. Dennis had got Derek Randall out and I'd got Dennis Amiss out. England was still in the ascendancy, but there was now a glimmer of hope, and I didn't want to drop a catch or make a mistake. So I said to Rod, 'Look, I'm going down to fine leg for a couple of overs. Look after things, I've got to have a break.' And I know Rod thinks I lost the plot, and maybe he's right. But I knew at the time it was something I had to do.

At tea England only had about 70 or 80 runs to get with five wickets in hand, but we persisted, the momentum swung back our way, and from a seemingly hopeless position we got them out and won the Centenary Test.

In the modern era the captain needs a lot of support, and nowadays people such as the vice-captain, coach, assistant coach, fitness advisers, statisticians and media advisers all assist to allow the captain to concentrate on the main aspects of the captaincy role.

Training captains

It has always surprised me that more time and effort isn't put into developing captains. How often do we hear apprehensive statements about a new captain? Why? Because there aren't adequate opportunities to learn and demonstrate leadership. Like batting, bowling and fielding, captaincy is a skill that has to be learnt. Traditionally, it has involved discussions around particular bowlers and standard field placings, but it is so much more. Respect from your team members, understanding different players' personalities and strengths, understanding your own strengths and weaknesses, and having good off-field support are not often discussed with new or even experienced captains. Training and developing captains (leaders) clearly has to remain a core teaching activity for coaches.

The core skills a captain needs to have are:

- leadership;
- acute situational and tactical awareness;
- good planning; and
- flexibility in decision making.

Encouraging the captain's role

Once the game begins the captain is responsible for what happens on the ground. Input from coaches and outside personnel may assist, but ultimately the captain is in charge. Pre-game and off-field planning needs to be flexible, designed so it encourages captains to read the play and use their intuition to make decisions. A coach who sits in the dressing room or on the boundary during a game and stifles a captain's decision making is neither constructive nor useful. Given that a major part of captaincy is responsibility, how do captains learn this if they are not allowed to make their own decisions, and make some mistakes?

Making mistakes

As we saw in chapter 4, making mistakes is a critical part of the learning process, so be prepared to make plenty of them. A captain will develop more quickly if he or she is not inhibited by the fear of making mistakes. Reflection and debriefing with the coach and other players is a far better way to help an inexperienced captain learn the role. Captaincy is not about right and wrong, it is about making decisions that are appropriate at a particular time.

Trusting the captain

Trusting and respecting a captain's decisions is extremely important. If the coach and administrators aren't able to do this, they had better pick another captain: they aren't on the ground when a potentially critical decision needs to be made — only the captain can make it.

Keeping captaincy in perspective

It's important as a captain to have routines and processes that allow you to take on the extra load, to get the concentration downtime and periods of relaxation required to be on your game for long periods.

Being confident and backing your judgement

Find the decision-making process that works for you. Be confident and back your judgement. If you think of something, do it immediately. The next ball or next over may be too late.

One of the great joys of captaincy is that no two days are the same. Different teams, different opponents, different conditions, a different attack, different batting line-up and different game situations make for a job that is both interesting and demanding. As with all Chappellway principles, the best way to learn it is to do it.

AN EXAMPLE OF AN EXCELLENT CAPTAIN — MY BROTHER IAN

My brother Ian was the best captain I played with or against. For me his example is the model for a quality captain.

Firstly, Ian was an excellent batsman so there was never an issue about his selection in the team. This point is very important. The approach that is sometimes used of selecting the captain for their captaincy skills when their batting skills are suspect can create problems within the team.

Secondly, Ian was decisive and fearless in his decision making. No one was spared the wrath of Ian if he thought it was justified for the good of the team. To him, it was a team game and the players had to play their part; but he always communicated individually with the players. Some didn't like his direct manner, but you always knew where you stood, and it was up to you to respond. Ian was greatly respected by his team as they knew he had our best interests at heart.

I'll never forget the test in Port-of-Spain, West Indies in 1973. On the last day the West Indies needed just 50 runs with 6 wickets in hand. We went to tea feeling pretty sorry for ourselves and the mood didn't change in the dressing-room. When we went back out on the ground Ian delivered a message to the team: that the match wasn't over and a quick wicket would turn the game. You could feel the mood lifting. As history shows, we got a wicket straight after tea, the West Indies panicked and we won the match. This was a perfect example of Ian's ability to work with people to get the best out of the team.

Scenario planning in captaincy

Here are three scenarios — three great battles of their day between bowlers and batters — that give an insight into the challenges of captaincy. In my experience the best captains are those who work as a team with their bowlers to plot the downfall of the opponents. Patience and planning along with a poker face are the tools of good captains. Once a captain shows his frustration or believes his team is beaten then you can rest assured that they will be.

1 Dennis Lillee versus Vivian Richards

Let's assume in this scenario that Viv Richards has just walked out to bat to face Dennis Lillee. This was always a fascinating contest because neither of these great players wanted to play second fiddle. As captain, it was my responsibility to work with Dennis to make sure we gave ourselves the best chance of getting Viv out early. From previous experience we both knew that Viv was extremely strong on his pads. Balls bowled even at off-stump would be worked through mid-wicket when Viv was hot. However, we also knew that this gave us a chance of dismissal if Dennis could bowl the ball just outside off stump and either run it away towards slips and get a catch behind, or jag one back for an LBW appeal. We all recognised that bowling short played Viv in, so it was important to get as many balls in the critical area while he was still settling in. That didn't mean that Dennis wouldn't bowl a bouncer every so often if Viv was looking comfortable on the front foot. Again, direction was important as bouncers had to be at least head height over off stump.

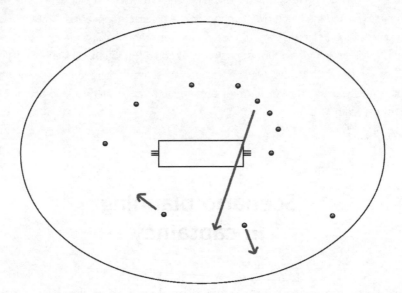

The field placement for Dennis Lillee versus Viv Richards early in his innings. The plan was to force Viv to hit straight down the ground or through the off side if he wanted runs, therefore maximising our chances of a catch in the slips. The arrows show the changes I would make to the field if Viv foiled any plans and settled in.

In his early days, Viv was predominantly a leg-side player. Any balls pitched on off stump were treated as though they had been pitched on leg stump for anyone else and were promptly dispatched in an arc from wide mid-on to backward square leg. Dennis and I decided that the best line for Viv was 15–20 centimetres outside the off stump to force him to play on the off side with a strong slip cordon. This tactic worked a treat for a while until Viv adapted and became equally proficient on the off side. The bad news was that he lost none of his ability on the leg side. We had just helped make him a better player!

We generally started with three slips, a gully, extra cover and mid-off on the off side, with a mid-on, mid-wicket and deep backward square leg, and bowled just outside off stump to him early. Once he settled, we generally shifted one of the slips into the cover region and may have considered dropping an extra man back on the leg side for the high bouncer over the middle stump. Some days it didn't matter what we tried, he was too good.

What Dennis and I were trying to do was force Viv to hit straight down the ground if he wanted runs, therefore maximising our chances of a catch into the slips. It was important as captain to monitor Dennis and make sure I didn't over-bowl him. Six overs of concentrated attack was generally the maximum before a bowling change.

2   Richard Hadlee versus Greg Chappell

In this scenario, let's assume that Richard Hadlee is bowling to me on a flat pitch and I'm going well and have made 60 runs. The ball is 45 overs old.

My great strength was my ability to drive. I liked to drive straight, and any ball pitched on leg stump would be dispatched through mid-wicket. I liked to cut when set, but favoured front-foot shots. So assuming I'm captain against myself, I would work with Richard to make sure he didn't over-pitch on the middle and leg or give me room outside off stump. I would direct him to work away just short of a length around off stump, while occasionally tempting me with an outswinger to cover drive. I would also suggest that every so often he give me a head-high bouncer over off-stump and let me have a go at the pull or hook shot.

The key would be patience, trying to keep me off strike and slow my scoring. In situations like this defence is often the best method of attack.

It would be very important for the bowlers to work as a unit, to keep me tied down. As captain I might bring up the third man into a third slip, and push the square leg more around into a mid-wicket, trying to dry up the runs while attacking with the three slips and the fine leg for the miscued hook. Even when bowling defensively a field needs to be set to maximise the limited wicket-taking opportunities.

Richard's fatigue would have to be taken into account, and the captain would have to decide who would replace him. You can see why the coach needs to train the captain and the players to deal with these sorts of situations.

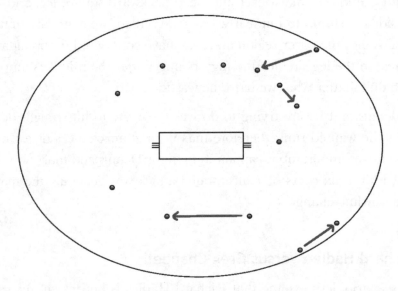

Field placement for Richard Hadlee versus Greg Chappell. Note the moves of third man to third slip, square leg to mid-wicket to dry up my strength on the on side, and a fine leg for the miscued hook.

3 Shane Warne versus Sachin Tendulkar

In this scenario, one of the great battles of the modern era, let's assume there's some spin in the wicket, although it's slow, and Sachin Tendulkar has just come to the crease.

Like the contest between Viv Richards and Dennis Lillee, this is a fascinating time for players and spectators. As captain, I know Shane is my strike bowler so I want to make sure he bowls as many balls at Sachin as possible. Therefore

I need to match up the bowling combination and field placements to ensure this occurs.

As a leg-spinner, Shane's primary ball turns to the off. I know from previous experience that Sachin will try and rock back on anything short, and place it through the off-side field. The dangers for Sachin are the drive through the mid-off and cover region, the possibility of a nick to the keeper or slips, and the ball that goes straight or turns back for an LBW shout.

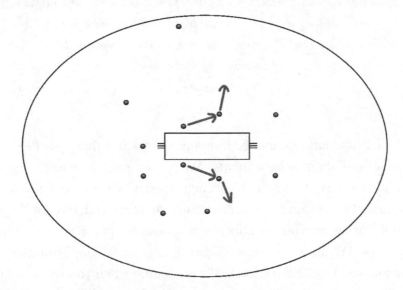

A typical field placement for Shane Warne versus Sachin Tendulkar, that is, for leg-spin bowling to a right-handed batter. One of the keys to captaincy is flexibility in decision making. Therefore, as captain the aim is to close off Sachin's preferred shots while having the best chance of getting him out. When he first comes to the wicket is the time to attack with close fielders on each side of the wicket. These fielders can be pushed back to catching fieldsmen on the drive, on each side of the wicket, or can be dropped back into the ring if he settles in.

Today, at first-class level, captains, players and coaches have the advantage of computer technology that allows them to create and work through different scenarios for different batters. These can be extremely useful tools, but they are only tools. The ability of the captain to understand the state of the play, to respond to the emotions of their players and to think outside the square at any given moment can never be replicated by a computer or statistics. Captaincy is a human skill that we need to develop and nurture.

Coaching

Any life can be damaged by the wrong words from the right person's lips.
Conversely, any life can be healed by the right words from the right person's
lips. Each of our lives has been touched by the presence of one individual
who made a tremendous difference. That individual may have trusted in you
when others doubted, backed you when others backed away, saw deeper into
your soul than you ever imagined possible. That person provided a
kind word at a critical moment, an encouraging smile,
or an arm around the shoulder.

ANON

It's my belief that nature intended humans to work together, to achieve and get enjoyment from their achievements. We're designed to learn, designed to teach, and designed to learn from each other. As we found in chapter 2, humans have large brains with an extensive memory capacity for the storage of ever-increasing amounts of information; we are exposed to endless learning opportunities. We always have, and can always make, opportunities to keep learning and teaching. Education really is exciting when you see it in this light and it's the way I suggest you approach your cricket and life generally. I believe that a majority of people understand this principle, subconsciously at least. This is why I advocate that coaches need to create stimulating and supportive learning environments where players can experience involvement, enjoyment, choice about the type of cricketer they want to be, the effectiveness of planning, motivation, awareness, and the result of all the above — achievement.

These are my coaching key words:

- involvement
- enjoyment
- choice
- planning
- motivation
- awareness
- achievement.

Creating an environment where players actually experience these emotions is not always easy, especially with large groups. It involves creativity and experimentation. But that's the fun of cricket. There are very few rights or wrongs in this world, just opportunities to try new ways and do it better.

Who's the boss, the coach or the captain?

As we discussed in the introduction, with full-time coaches being so involved in training programs and team development, you could well ask, 'Where does the coach's job stop and the captain's begin?' In my view the coach should work behind the scenes as an educator, nurturer and mentor, while the captain devises the game plan and tactics used during the game. Naturally, in good positive relationships the captain and coach work together on the game plan and discuss tactics during the match, but from my point of view those are the basic parameters.

As coach of the Southern Redbacks my role was the development and preparation of the team. I would develop training programs, manage player development, and plan and run practice. Once game day started I was a spectator — the captain took over. That was my relationship with Darren Lehmann and Greg Blewett. During practice they both wanted to get on with their preparation, so I was the boss; but once game day came, I moved into the background and whichever one was captain became the boss. My job was then to support them in every way possible. We had a good rapport and a very positive relationship.

I do not believe that a coach should get involved in what's happening on the field. You're a sounding board. From time to time you see things that are obviously not working, so during a break you might approach the captain and say, 'This is not working too well, what do you think about this?' If, however, your rapport with the captain is not well developed, try other ways of getting your point across. It's important to be sensitive to the situation and have a 'feel' for when the time is right. Remember situational awareness? It applies to coaches too. There are a number of ways of getting through. Try talking to one of the senior team members the captain respects: 'I've been watching what's happening; why don't you suggest to [the captain]...' Or simply sit back and wait until the captain comes to you. The way you communicate depends on your relationship with and understanding of each other. That's why it's so important that it's a positive and trusting one.

One of the dangers of the modern game is that some coaches want to be part of on-field decision making. There have even been proposals for radio devices so that the coach can communicate to the captain and batters direct. As I said, I believe it's wrong. If we are trying to develop captains to be leaders, cricketers to be leaders, they've got to be allowed to make their own decisions. It's only by making decisions and mistakes that they learn and grow. Besides, there is plenty of time at the lunch or tea break to discuss tactics. The issue of how we teach, how we learn, how we develop and have trust in our leaders is critical; it's fundamental to the game and its survival in the twenty-first century.

The role of coaches and administrators is essentially to be educators, mentors and managers (organisers).

Communication

Being a good communicator is an essential prerequisite for coaching, and that means understanding your players. Here are some important things coaches and administrators need to know about them:

- their individuality;
- their strengths and weaknesses;
- what motivates them;
- the best way to communicate to them;
- when stress, fatigue or personal problems are affecting their game;
- their health; and
- their goals and plans.

The way you speak and react to your players, both verbally and non-verbally, is another important key. Remember that people tend to form judgements about each other within seconds of their meeting, so first impressions *are* important. And be prepared to listen, then offer feedback. These are the things I've found that help me communicate to my players.

Talent identification, selection and development

Being able to assess talent and potential talent is another of the coach's important roles — it affects the performance of the team now and in the future. Because cricket is such a complex game, talent identification can require a greater understanding of an individual's level of development and potential for improvement than is needed in many other sports. Players tend to develop over a lengthy period and often not to any particular pattern. Some mature earlier, some later. Neil Harvey was a mature cricketer at nineteen years of age when he went away with the 1948 Australian team, while Bob Simpson, though he played for New South Wales as a teenager, did not start making centuries for Australia in test cricket until he was much older. Sachin Tendulkar was making test centuries for India at an age when most cricketers are concerned with whether they can get into their school's first eleven. Because of these irregularities in development, you may need to make decisions about the potential of individual players over a number of seasons. Think about where they are on *their* developmental calendar. If you can, put flexible structures in place to deal with this. Having the ability to recognise and nurture cricket talent has become more and more important as other sports and pastimes tap into cricket's traditional source of players.

> **WHEN CONSIDERING A PLAYER'S LEVEL OF DEVELOPMENT, ASK YOURSELF QUESTIONS SUCH AS:**
>
> - What's the player's age in terms of their sporting development (training age)?
> - Is their real age relevant?
> - Is the player being assessed on current ability rather than their long-term potential?
> - Have we watched the player long enough and know them well enough to gauge their potential?
> - Will they develop quickly or over the longer term?
> - Have they had appropriate competitive experiences?
> - Is there something other than cricket holding back their progress?

The answers you come up with can depend on all sorts of things: the person's age, the errors they make that hold them back, their ability to learn and apply their learning, how they deal with stress or outside influences. That's why it's very important to base your judgements on several different situations over a period of time. In fact, this is the only way to gain an understanding of the individual and gauge their potential.

Concurrent to the talent selection process is the selection and nurturing process. Issues to consider include:

- choosing the right time to select a player;
- deciding where to use them in the team;
- deciding how best to handle them during times of poor form and personal problems; and
- working out how to nurture the player to fulfil their potential.

There are also a number of 'bigger' picture issues, including

- team dynamics;
- team development; and
- team goals.

These are all issues for coaches, selectors and administrators to grapple with. Coaching, developing and nurturing young people's potential in the game is a very involved process, but also tremendously rewarding. It's one of the keystones of leadership — of captaincy, coaching and administration.

Coaching the individual

I'm always searching for a greater understanding of the processes of learning and teaching. When I was young my father and mother provided me with a fantastic environment for learning to play cricket — though my love for learning cricket didn't translate to the classroom. I was the kind of kid who used to like diving in and getting his hands dirty, and without this kind of stimulation I would quickly lose interest in what my teachers were explaining. Unfortunately, not one of them got me excited about the subject they were teaching.

I use this example to highlight the fact that we are all different in our personalities and our learning styles. The coach works with all sorts of personalities: naturally talented players who are disruptive, obstinate players, talented players who lack in confidence, and team players. The joys and frustrations of working with players can never be underestimated. Enjoy the process and embrace the challenge. If you respect the individuals in your team, the changes you make will be positive.

GOOD COACHING — THE RISE AND RISE OF VIV RICHARDS

When Viv Richards first came onto the scene, he ran us all out in the World Cup with his fantastic fielding, and he was also obviously a batsman of rare talent. In the First Test at the Gabba ground in Brisbane, Viv went out cheaply fending outside the off stump to Gary Gilmour, our left-arm opening bowler. Viv really struggled up until the Third Test in Melbourne, where he opened the batting and made a couple of forties. The rest is history. He made a hundred in one of the remaining tests and went to England in the Australian winter and made over 800 runs in the series. In his excellent book *Winning Ways*, Rudi Webster reveals how Viv would be so wound up and anxious before he went out to bat that by the time he got to the middle he was a physical wreck. The decision was taken to allow him to open the batting and thus relieve him of this unproductive downtime. Also, and more importantly, Rudi worked with Viv to develop a simple routine to concentrate on when it was his turn to bat. This involved two thought processes: firstly, making sure he focused on the ball from the time the bowler turned at the top of his mark; and secondly, allowing his feet to move. These triggers allowed Viv to block out all the distractions and allowed him time to settle in. Rudi also had Viv do some exercises before he went in to bat, which also helped to relieve some of the build-up of tension. Viv's preference was to do some skipping. Rudi Webster's action represents high-quality coaching; for cricket lovers all over the world it was well worth the effort.

Coaching the team

There's an old saying, so old that I don't think anyone remembers who coined it, but it's very true: A champion team will always beat a team of champions.

Moulding your side into a group of players who support each other, who put the team before their own personal gain, and who work together setting and achieving team goals, is the number one priority for any coach. Take a minute to revisit the 'team before me' attitude we discussed at the beginning of the chapter. It was all about working together to set goals and achieve them. Like the development of an individual, the development of the team into a smooth functioning group is an ever-evolving process. Think about this point and whether it's part of your coaching program.

Many of our most successful companies and businesses use team development programs designed to build teamwork in departments, or groups who play specific roles within a department. The reason behind this is that by having dynamic groups and teams consisting of individuals all working together for a common cause, efficiency and productivity improve. This results in a heightened feeling of achievement for the group (or team) which in turn rubs off on the individuals. Greater productivity produces higher profits, which in the end means better career opportunities for the individuals. The process builds a feeling of 'belonging', with everyone a winner.

I'm not saying that you should rush out and grab a management consultant to introduce group dynamics into your cricket team, but I believe it's worth reading up on material that offers ideas and makes you aware of the things you can do to develop teamwork.

Try these resources for a start:

- John Wooden, *Wooden: A Lifetime of Observations and Reflections On and Off the Court* (Contemporary Books, 1997), or log on to his website www.coachwooden.com. John is a highly successful basketball coach.
- Joe Torres, *Ground Rules for Winners: 12 Keys to Managing Team Players, Tough Bosses, Setbacks and Success* (Hyperion, 1999). Joe was the coach of the New York Yankees.
- Noel M. Tichy & Stratford Sherman, *Control Your Destiny or Someone Else Will* (HarperBusiness, 2001). Lessons in mastering change, the principles of Jack Welch who revolutionised General Electric.

Keep your mind open to new and better ways of developing teamwork and team spirit. The rewards will be more than you ever imagined.

Finding the key learning moment

Every person I have ever met has a 'hot spot' — that is, a situation and a moment in time when they are at their most receptive for learning. A coach or administrator must be able to understand the individual in order to recognise these learning moments and unlock the player's potential. This doesn't only apply to cricket: it applies to any learning and developmental situation.

Here's a checklist that coaches and administrators can use to learn to understand their players:

- Get to know the player and engage with them.

- Understand as much as you can about their cultural and home life.

- Use the player's existing knowledge or preconceptions as a starting point for moving forward or learning something new.

- Monitor the player's progress. Let them know you're watching their development and seeing improvement, and that you care.

- Encourage players to help each other — there's nothing like learning from a peer.

Fear and failure

Research indicates that we learn best either when we are strongly motivated to pursue a goal or when we're exposed to a situation that generates a strong emotional reaction such as fear or failure. This is because excitement and danger cause hormone releases in the body that trigger strong memories of the events concerned. Therefore, any new situation has the potential to result in learning. However, fear and failure can also cause problems. When the fear and failure emotions are the primary long-term source of learning, the body will attempt to protect itself and redirect its attention from productive learning. There's a fine balance.

It's very important to be aware of this phenomenon of human behaviour. Be aware of situations like the following:

- fear of going out cheaply as you're waiting to bat (as happened to Viv Richards);

- fear of being injured;

- fear of not meeting others' or your own expectations;

- anxiety engendered by a certain player or opposition;

- if you're a spinner, fear about being belted around the park;

- if you're a quick, fear about not being able to control the ball;

- if you're a keeper, fear about missing catches and stumpings.

Be sensitive to the above emotions in your players. Help them if they're fearful of failing. These fears must be overcome for a cricketer to reach their full potential. Cricket should never be disruptive or life-threatening emotionally. It is a game where competing against each other creates excitement and fun, and competition also gives feedback about our progress. Sure, we'll all get nervous, but only because we want to do well. It shouldn't be because our coach or family will disown us if we don't. This is why I place so much emphasis on the creative and supportive learning environment. Catch the players doing good things; this is important.

Encouraging leadership throughout the team

While one player should always have the ultimate say, the development of decision making in all team members should be encouraged: it creates good teams. By helping players assume responsibility administrators, coaches and captains will enhance their players' understanding of cricket and enhance the future of the game. Players should be encouraged to take on as much responsibility as they can handle.

IF IT IS TO BE, IT IS UP TO ME

Many years ago I saw a short motivational video in which Reggie Jackson, the New York Yankees' power hitter, spoke of the need for each player to take responsibility for the team performance. We were playing the mighty West Indies in Australia at the time so I decided to incorporate Reggie's philosophy into our team ethic. As a group we talked about the need for each of us to 'stand up and be counted' a few times each during the series if we were to hold off the marauders from the Caribbean.

If each one of us could take a turn at being the one to bowl a good spell or share a telling partnership, or be the one to effect a run-out or take a good catch, we had a better chance of stopping the world champions from continuing their winning way. The West Indian team under Clive Lloyd is one of the most awesome that I have seen, but it was interesting to see how much more cohesive our performance became when we took turns at taking on the responsibility for our performance. Rather than leaving it up to a few of the senior players most of the time, everyone did a little bit more and we found it easier to focus on the process of playing to our potential.

We finished up drawing the series against the West Indies, thanks to an even team performance plus some stand-out performances from Kim Hughes, Allan Border and John Dyson with the bat, and Dennis Lillee and Bruce Yardley with the ball.

The concept of all team members taking their turn to be the one to make a difference is a concept that all teams can use no matter what the level of competition.

Coaching juniors

With junior cricket becoming increasingly structured, coaching has become extremely important in the development of young people. The quickest and easiest way for a coach to succeed is to get their players to succeed at what they're trying to do. You'll recall the example of the Sydney girls school. The girls had been floundering and frustrated, but when they were allowed to concentrate solely on hitting the ball, suddenly they tasted success and enjoyment. The following three steps will help you achieve success in coaching juniors.

Step 1 — Hitting and bowling

The first step is to start hitting and bowling the ball consistently. This is the first thing you want a young cricketer to learn when they first pick up a bat. Say to them, 'Okay, don't try and hit it too hard, just hit it. Slow your movements down a bit and watch the ball from the time it leaves my hand and make sure you hit it. The power will come when your timing gets better.' With bowling it's similar. Make sure they don't try and bowl too fast or bowl the types of deliveries that just make it too hard for them. Get them to bowl naturally, at a comfortable pace, and concentrate on accuracy. If a kid bowls straight at the stumps you'll be surprised how many wickets they will get.

Step 2 — Fun and a sense of belonging

The second step is about having fun and achieving a sense of belonging. To make sure this happens, rotate the batting and bowling order so everyone gets a turn. Also rotate the captaincy; it is too early to be specialising. Obviously the coach will do most of the decision making for the very young ones, but encourage them to make some of the decisions themselves. Be creative and work within their level of competence. Remember, winning's not everything. What's important is making sure that kids feel they belong to the team and learn to love, respect and have passion for the game. We don't want any more horror stories like the one I told you in chapter 3, about the poor kid who'd been waiting to bat for two weeks only to be run out first ball — from the non-striker's end!

Step 3 — Caring, teamwork and skills

The third step is to show them that you care, and build teamwork and skills.

Look after the players. Work on team spirit. Emphasise what I call the 'macro' elements of batting, bowling and fielding, not the 'micro' elements.

As a batter, the macro elements are:

- Watch the ball.
- Hit the ball, don't try to hit it too hard.

As a bowler, the macro elements are:

- Bowl at a comfortable pace.
- Concentrate on bowling straight.

As a fielder, the macro elements are:

- Be alert and ready to move fast.
- Watch the batter for early cues.
- Make your throws efficient and user-friendly for the receiver.

The 'micro' elements are those fine details of movement that should not be emphasised at this stage:

- Keep your left elbow up.
- Bend your front knee.
- Step to the ball.
- In bowling, keep your front arm up.

The micro elements have no purpose at the junior level. In fact, these elements force kids to use their forebrain, their conscious mind, instead of their subconscious. Once they're thinking consciously about what they're doing, their motor skills won't work effectively — and then the macro elements won't work because they're too busy worrying about the micro things. It's a vicious circle. Encourage the players to focus on the macro things and the brain will sort out the micro things. This is so important that I can't overemphasise it!

A player's subconscious will sort it out much better than a coach will ever do.

Coaching batting

My coaching approach looks at the batter's performance and works to improve it within the context of the process of batting. As we discussed in the section 'Training for batting' in chapter 3, it is a reactive process. It's also an intermittent, high-speed activity. Even if you run three it's only thirty seconds from start to finish. Batting relies on conscious decision making up until the bowler's delivery stride, but then it relies on subconscious decision making for body movement and striking the ball. Conscious decision making takes over again for running. This is followed by a period of recuperation. Sports scientists call this type of activity the phosphate–creatine system.

Coaching the whole movement

We discussed in chapter 1 how the batting action is a whole movement. It's not something you can dissect. The unweighting, coiling, balance and timing are all interdependent and it's best to let the subconscious take care of them. In fact, batting movements have to be subconscious to be effective. If batting movements are conscious performance will be inconsistent.

The danger in learning or modifying parts of the stroke by methods such as repetitive drills is that they could adversely effect the desired goal. If you do need to modify part of a player's batting movement, immediately work it back into the whole movement. See the golfing example on pages 107–108 in chapter 3.

Emphasise the macro elements:

- watching the bowler for cues as they run in;
- applying fierce focus to the bowler's hand on delivery;
- unweighting correctly; and
- making the conscious intention to move towards the ball then let the subconscious take over.

Correcting a problem

The most effective way of creating change is 'subconscious training'. This is done by progressively changing the stimulus. Here's an example. In teaching or modifying a batter's square cut the coach may limit the area where the ball should be hit. Remember target practice? If you don't, check it out on pages 79–81. It forces the batter to adjust their whole movement regime, not just the wrists or the back-lift, etc. This way the batter is playing the shot naturally and in the most fluid way that their physique allows. A trick I use is to make sure the batter has some success by bowling in such a way that it allows them to hit the ball easily. Once they get the hang of it I progressively increase the variables. This way, without having said anything, the batter corrects the problem his/herself. I find this creates strong coach/player relationships based on a two-way process of exploration and learning. This is one of the real joys of coaching.

The training session

I make sure there is a definite plan and form to the training session that I relate to the players at the start. Ask them to have a plan too so that they get the most out of the session. Stimulate improvement in the players by testing them against different players in different situations. This gives them a challenge but also the opportunity for success and improvement. When they're ready, move them up a notch and put them against players of better ability. The aim is to give them a taste of success to build confidence followed by the next challenge. Integrate fitness training and batting, bowling and fielding practice as much as possible with net practice, and where practicable end the session with a simulated match. This trains the brain to apply learning (training) to competitive cricket: hard fought matches where batters have to develop a level of expertise to counter the bowlers, fielders and pitch will always be the ultimate way to train.

Game preparation

I strongly encourage coaches to help their players learn techniques for dealing with stress, and visualization, to help them prepare for a game.

Talk to the player about identifying signs of stress — sensing changes in heartbeat, tension in the neck and shoulder areas, rigid movements, and trouble in concentrating. Stress can be relieved by the coach and the player working together and developing routines, as Rudi Webster did with Viv Richards (see page 193).

The use of visualisation in the overall training program can provide the player with greater self-understanding, learning recall and performance. When Bradman referred to how great batters had plenty of time to play the ball, he was highlighting the fact that they had come close to perfecting the movement patterns necessary to maximise the response to the ball bowled. Visualisation can really assist in perfecting movement patterns. If I was going to be facing Joel Garner tomorrow I would sit down today and, in a relaxed state, visualise the ground, my routine, Joel running in to bowl, the cues I have developed from previous experience, the type of ball, and my response. I may go through this process four or five times with different bowlers, different deliveries and the different end results I wanted to create. I always did this to train my nervous system how to respond. I found it was a fantastic help. Encourage your players to use these methods in preparing for a game.

Coaching bowling

I've been lucky to face many great bowlers: Dennis Lillee, Andy Roberts, John Snow, Joel Garner, Derek Underwood, Lance Gibbs and Abdul Qadir, to name a few. As well, I've had the opportunity to study the likes of Shane Warne, Courtney Walsh and Muttiah Muralitharan in action. They all displayed a great love of the art of bowling and all were caught up in the endeavour of mastering this great activity.

In coaching bowling there are four things I concentrate on:

- spinal integrity;
- a fluid and reproducible action and delivery;
- training — perfecting by doing; and
- taking wickets.

Spinal integrity

Bowling is an extremely physical activity. It requires a lot of energy and strength and places great strain on the body's muscles, joints and ligaments over an extended period. So, as a coach, if I see aspects of a bowler's delivery that I believe will cause injury at some point, as I did with Jason Gillespie (see page 27), I work with them to modify the way they bowl. Otherwise I leave the bowler's natural action alone.

The most common cause of injury is lack of spinal integrity. Let me explain what this means. The two points at which the bowler's body is under most stress are (a) when the back foot lands, and (b) when the front foot lands. At these two points it is critical that the bowler's spine is aligned, because if it is compromised the enormous pressure placed on the spine at these moments can cause severe injury. (For more detail see page 118.)

Observe the delivery strides of your players and see whether you can detect any problems in the spine at these two points. Inappropriate swivelling or sliding of the feet during the delivery strides are a good clue to instability. Sports science indicates that a flexed and rotated spine at these points is a major problem. If you notice this in any of your bowlers, or you have a bowler who is regularly breaking down, check the run-up before you do anything else. Often the micro problems can be overcome be dealing with the macro problems. If in doubt please get expert advice. You might save your bowler's career.

A fluid reproducible action and delivery

Instil among your bowlers the need to have a reproducible action that produces consistent deliveries. We discussed this in detail in 'Training for bowling' on pages 111–120. Bowlers must be able to control the direction and length in order to build a repertoire (an arsenal) of balls. That is, they must be able to control their bowling to the extent that they can decide what type of ball they will bowl to the batter and then deliver it. This is one of the keys to the success of bowlers like Glenn McGrath and Shane Warne. They've decided as they turn to come into bowl what type of ball it's going to be and where it's going to land — and it happens nine times out of ten.

Training — perfecting by doing

There's a theory held by many coaches that restricts the amount of bowling a bowler does. The theory is that bowling puts a lot of stress on the body and therefore by restricting the amount of bowling you lengthen the bowler's career. The problem with this theory is how you become a good bowler if you restrict your training time. Quite simply, I don't think you can. To develop your consistency and weaponry in bowling you need to practice and practice. The bowler's body should withstand the strain provided their movements don't put undue pressure on joints and muscles, and that there is spinal integrity through the run-up and at the point of delivery.

I'm not saying that bowlers shouldn't do various fitness and strengthening exercises to strengthen their bodies for the job. But again, I would advise that you try to incorporate fitness and strengthening work into the overall training program as much as possible so the brain can reapply it to the bowling action.

Taking wickets

Don Bradman made the point in his classic book *The Art of Cricket* that bowlers win matches by taking wickets. So, just as scoring runs is the ultimate goal of the batter, the bowler's goal is to get the batters out. This is the fundamental battle on the cricket field and why bowler–batter scenarios such as Shane Warne versus Sachin Tendulkar create such interest for cricket lovers all over the world. It's like two super-warriors in mortal combat until one wins and the other dies.

The bowler's advantage is that batters make mistakes, so it's important that they develop the ability to set the batter up for their demise. This is where the reproducible action and ball comes into play — it sets up a false feeling of security in the batter which the bowler can then take advantage of. The bowler's repertoire has a number of deliveries that look similar, but are in fact different. Coaches need to help their bowlers develop a number of deceptive ploys to outsmart the batter.

Finally, bowlers need to be helped to understand that they have no control over the batter's response. Once the ball has left the bowler's hand there is nothing the bowler can do — except think tactically about the next ball.

Remind your bowlers that they have the opportunity to seize control of the match, and there can be no greater reward.

Coaching wicket-keeping and fielding

I like to do fun things and challenging things with fielding. As kids we used to go to the local oval, where there was a hand-roller for rolling the wicket. We'd pull the roller out from the shed onto the oval and throw balls so they skim off it to the kid standing on the other side. We would stand either end of the roller and throw balls across it from end to end. If you hit the top of the roller it would shoot straight through, but if you hit down the sides a bit it would shoot off to the side. It was similar to the old slips cradles, which are also good fun. We'd choose partners and have two sides, like doubles in tennis, and the first team to drop three lost. So of course, as kids, we would throw the ball harder and harder to make it more and more difficult and sometimes you'd miss the roller; you'd lose a point for that.

As coach I introduced these sorts of 'fielding games' to the Southern Redbacks. From time to time when we'd be nearing the end of a training session I'd say, 'Okay, pick a partner, we're going to have a catching contest.' And we had some fantastic contests! All the batters would be trying to avoid the bowlers because the batters reckoned the bowlers couldn't catch as well. But the bowlers would say, 'We'll show them, let's go.' The bowlers would often win against the odds and they'd get really pumped up, knocking off the batters. Fun like this is critical to the learning process.

The smart coach is the one who makes sure it doesn't get out of hand, that they're not throwing the ball too hard, because then it becomes dropping practice. There's nothing worse when a team is supposed to be doing catching practice than having the player who's hitting the balls smashing them, trying to make the fielders drop catches. That's not catching practice. You've got to make sure the standard is commensurate with the talents of the players and that somebody is supervising it so that nobody gets hurt or loses confidence. You don't want your players dropping a lot of catches in training because that destroys their self-esteem and their confidence.

When I first started coaching at South Australia there was a bowler by the name of Mark Harrity. He was a good athlete but a fairly ordinary outfielder, so I spent some time with him. I started off hitting him lobs, fairly easy balls, so he could actually catch them and experience a bit of success. And I remember one of our players pulling me aside one day and saying, 'That's no good, trouble is he can catch those but he drops the hard ones. You make him run, make him catch them on the run.' And I said, 'Well, I'm not sure that's the best way to go. I think I've got to take him in stages. I've got to build his confidence first before I start stretching him out. If I stretch him out before his confidence is up he's going to drop them and all that's going to do is drive his confidence further down.' By the end of the season Mark's confidence had grown so much that, together with his natural athleticism, he was running 30 metres and taking catches nobody else would have even got to. Because we built his confidence up at practice, he now believed he could catch the ball in a match, and he did. For the next three seasons he didn't drop one catch. And in fact he took quite a number of spectacular ones — screamers on the run. It was a great result for Mark, and a great result for the team. It also reaffirmed to me the importance of building confidence.

To me, that's what coaching's about: recognising the level that the individual is at, pitching his training at that level, rather than treating everyone the same.

The frustrated coach — what to do in times of despair

Sometimes, no matter what you do, you just can't work out what's going on with your players. One moment they're on fire and the next moment they seem woeful. My advice is to go back and work through the fundamentals:

- the core principles of movement;
- preparation and visualization;

- attitude;
- concentration and stress; and
- fitness.

Here are some scenarios I'm sure you've come across and some suggestions of how to counteract the problems.

Why is it that some days they play well and others they're terrible?

Unweighting the body correctly is crucial to success. By not understanding the need to unweight their body correctly, most batters reduce the options available for responding to what the bowler has initiated. Consequently they are inconsistent. Because they do not unweight properly, especially when anxious, they are particularly vulnerable early in their innings. Incorrect initial movements increase the likelihood of low scores. Once they have survived the initial anxiety period many players relax and begin to move better. This is usually the day they play their best. Until they understand the principle of unweighting, that is, loading one leg at a time, they tend to commit their weight inefficiently prior to establishing the line and length of the delivery. They reduce the options available to them and stop tracking the ball in flight. Any success they have is purely accidental.

The other side to the problem of consistency is planning, mental preparation and focus — and how to do their job in the game within the overall team plan. A lot of modern coaching exacerbates this problem because players are not being coached to work through the problems for themselves; they are being coached to rely on someone else to do that for them. If cricketers are developed to be self-aware and self-reliant other results should become more consistent.

They have got no idea of playing the ball off their legs

If players don't unweight properly, particularly if they commit significant weight to one leg, usually the front leg, they are unable to adjust to the demands of the delivery without overbalancing. Once the balance has been impinged the quality of the shot will be negatively affected. By timing the initial movement and unweighting properly the player will track the ball longer and will have a greater range of options available to them.

Why can't they play off the back foot?

Most players unweight improperly and usually commit to the front foot before line and length are determined. Once committed to the front foot they are unable to push back onto the back foot. All they can do is lift the body up and fend off the ball with their arms. This will often lead to disaster as balls are fended off to close catchers in front of the bat or into the gully or slip cordon.

If we could only stop them bowling down the leg side!

Balance and correct unweighting are as important for a bowler as they are for a batter. Most bowlers are so enthusiastic that they generally try to bowl too fast and throw themselves off balance. As they fall away to the off side the body's counteracting mechanism will cause them to push the ball to the leg side. By showing them the correct way to unweight for their style we should be able to help them to improve their accuracy and produce a consistent performance.

It is as if they are scared when the ball is hit hard at them!

They probably are scared. By showing fielders the correct position to get into as the batsman is about to strike the ball, we will increase their chance of stopping and/or catching the ball. Most fielders have no idea of what to watch for in order to get early signals, or how to unweight themselves properly for early preparation. Again, if we can show them what to look for and how to unweight their body appropriately they will be better equipped to respond to balls hit in their direction.

Coaching for the love of it

The concept of education, which in effect is what coaching is about, comes from the Latin word 'educere' meaning 'to draw out'. Too many of us, as coaches, get caught up wanting to do things a certain way rather than working together with our players to help them move forward. This inflexibility prevents two-way exploration of the player's performance (called 'symmetrical' in two-way communication theory), whereby they slowly take responsibility for their own problem solving. When you look at it this way, coaching is the art of becoming redundant! Jokes aside, there is a lot of satisfaction in seeing your players improve their performance.

Sometimes coaching can be very frustrating. Getting communication going with some players can feel like it's taking a lifetime. Creating trust can be hard too. But don't be put off. In time it will happen. One aspect you *do* have control over is your coaching environment. You can turn that into anything you want. It doesn't matter if your practice facilities and equipment aren't brilliant.

New bats and balls and all the latest training gear aren't the keys to success. The environment you create — a fun environment with great team spirit, trust and respect, and with everyone wanting to learn and better themselves — is the key to success.

When I was coaching the Southern Redbacks, we were in Tasmania at one stage, and just for a change, we went out on the middle of the ground and played a game of beach cricket. We didn't have any boundaries — the players could hit the ball anywhere they liked, they could run seven if they wanted to. And it was interesting how much freer they played — batting, bowling and fielding. They stopped thinking about what they were doing; they just watched the ball and hit it as far as they could. They didn't worry about hitting it on the ground either; they were hitting it over the field. You see, there was no fear attached and it was fun. Young kids respond to this sort of training really well. But even 'old kids' respond to it too. I played in the game as well and had a ball — it was fantastic. It was a good fun session and we need to do more of it, particularly with the younger kids coming through. Take away the boundaries, take away the rules, take away the restrictions, take away the fear. Introduce the fun, introduce the freedom, watch them grow. And let me tell you, they'll grow quickly. I believe that's the art of coaching.

THE LIGHTHOUSE

When I was coaching the Southern Redbacks, the life coach, Carol Fox, came to talk to us about team building and life performance. She gave me this piece called 'The Lighthouse' which I believe is particularly relevant to coaching.

The metaphor is a lighthouse. The lighthouse is anchored on the rock, no matter where it is built. Sometimes the lighthouse is rebuilt in other areas as the weather and conditions change — same lighthouse, same lighthouse keeper, always anchored in the rock. The lighthouse is there to do one thing, and that is to shine the light. The purpose of the light is often varied. Sometimes it's a warning, sometimes it's there to attract attention, and sometimes it's there to guide. Whatever the purpose, it's always anchored in the rock. Those who built and operate the lighthouse know something that the others do not: they know where the rocks are — where the trouble is — and they are there to guide others around these things.

When the light is able to help steer ships into the harbour safely, the lighthouse keeper rejoices! When this happens, however, the lighthouse keeper does not go over and have a party with the captain of the ship. Instead, the keeper silently rejoices and continues to shine the light. Most captains who reach port safely due to the light of the lighthouse never know the lighthouse keeper. The lighthouse keeper doesn't publish a statement telling others that he saved a ship! He is silent and continues, often alone, anchored in the rock.

For those ships that did not look up to see the lighthouse, and who wound up on the rocks in disaster, the lighthouse keeper may be saddened. But the lighthouse keeper does not go over to rescue the ship. The lighthouse keeper does not take responsibility for those who end up on the rocks! The lighthouse keeper does not go into depression about the event and dismantle the lighthouse due to the ship that didn't look to see the light. No. Instead, the lighthouse has one purpose, and that is to shine the light, shine the light, and shine the light.

Do not take responsibility for those who do not heal. Don't take responsibility for those who do. Celebrate those who heal, cry over the ones that don't, but don't take responsibility for anything but the integrity of the energy you put out. Shine the light and stay in place. Continue to anchor yourself in the rock of wisdom, and do constant maintenance on the purity of the light that you display.

The five pathways to success revisited

When you read something, go to a movie, learn something, watch television or listen a radio program, it's always a good idea to summarise what you saw or learnt. Sometimes it might just be a mental summary, sometimes the book or DVD is more complex and you might need to write it down.

So let's recap the five pathways to becoming a successful cricketer.

The core principles of movement

By watching the 23 best cricketers of the modern era we discovered a revolutionary movement regime. What did they all have in common? They all understood, if even subconsciously, the natural laws of physics as they apply to the human body — that is, *unweighting, coiling, using levers* and *timing*.

The brain

Understanding the fundamentals of how this enormously complex human organ works helps us to understand the way our memory and nervous system combine for good decision making and efficient movement. It also explains why the subconscious is such an important part of success in cricket.

A creative and supportive learning environment

The unstructured learning environment, the learning environment of so many of our great cricketers over the last one and a quarter centuries of cricket, allows the young player to develop naturally and play according to their physique, temperament and ability. It also 'bombards' the subconscious with a huge range of experiences, creating a virtual databank of memories which the player then uses to outplay their opponents. This was my learning environment: having supportive parents, and playing with friends in the backyard, at the park and on the beach.

Organising yourself for success

If you don't have a goal, how do you measure whether you're successful or not? All the successful people I know, whether their success is in sport, business or the community, organise themselves for success. They have routines in which they:

- set goals and achieve them step by step;
- have a positive attitude and are confident;
- concentrate effectively for long periods;
- are healthy;
- are fit;
- are tactically and situationally aware;
- reflect on their performance and ways of doing what they want to achieve; and
- develop as a person outside their chosen field.

Having these routines will enable you to use your natural talent to achieve your full potential.

Leadership

Leadership is not just for captains, coaches and administrators, it's for every single team member. Leadership is about teamwork, having ideas, articulating and evaluating them, and following through. Good leadership encourages others to grow. Captains need to display this leadership, as well as have acute situational and tactical awareness, good planning skills and flexibility in decision-making. The coach's role is to educate, mentor and nurture, to make a positive difference to their players both on and off the field. Remember the Latin word that forms the root of educate: *educere* — to draw out.

In October 2003, just before the Indian team toured Australia, the Indian captain Sourav Ganguly arranged to come and see me about his batting. The champion Australian team was expected to win the series easily, but as we know the series was a draw and India retained the Border–Gavaskar trophy. In fact, the scoreboard tells us that India all but won. Sourav and I spent an intensive week together in Sydney where I explained our five pathways to becoming a successful cricketer while we worked on his batting. Sourav was interested in them all, but particularly in the Core Principles of Movement, organising yourself for success and leadership.

Sourav has kindly agreed to take up the story from his point of view. I think it shows that by embracing the five pathways your whole approach to the game can change for the better, driving you ever closer to your full potential:

In the winter before the 2003–04 test series against Australia, I flew to Sydney to spend a week with Greg Chappell. I was trying to improve my own game and I was also looking for some ways in which we could beat the world champion Australian team. Greg and I worked on my batting: a few technical things and how I approached it too — what was going on in my mind when I was batting. Greg told me that footwork was a product of the mind and that you needed to clear your mind to be able to make the right moves back and forward. It helped me a lot and I batted much better throughout the Australian tour.

But we also talked about many other things, including his five pathways to cricketing success. And I was interested to know all about them. Mostly we discussed things like how you organise yourself for success and leadership. It was fascinating and I believe it contributed a lot towards my performance as a player and a captain, and India's success in Australia. As history shows, we retained the Border–Gavaskar trophy and were unlucky not to win the series outright.

SOURAV GANGULY

BIBLIOGRAPHY

Sporting expertise

Starkes, J. & Ericsson, K. A, *Expert Performance in Sports*, Human Kinetics, 2003.

Learning and teaching

Andrisani, J., *Think Like a Tiger: An Analysis of the Tiger Woods' Mental Game*, Putnam, 2002.

Bransford, J., Brown, A. L. & Cocking, R., *How People Learn: Brain, Mind, Experience and School*, National Academy of Sciences, 2000.

Callwey, W. T., *The Inner Game of Golf*, Pan, 1979.

Colwin, C. M, *Breakthrough Swimming*, Human Kinetics, 2002.

Greenfield, S., *Brain Story*, BBC Worldwide, 2000.

King, I., *Winning and Losing, Losing and Winning: Lessons from a Decade Physically Preparing the Elite Athletes*, 2nd edition, Kings Sports, 2002.

Krebs, C. & Brown J., *A Revolutionary Way of Thinking*, Hill of Content, 1998.

Linksman, R., *How To Learn Anything Quickly: Accelerated Program for Rapid Learning*, Coral Publishing Group, 1996.

McLoughlin, C., 'The Implications of the Research Literature on Learning Styles for the Design of Instructional Material', *Australian Journal of Educational Technology*, 15(3), 1999, pp. 222–41.

O'Brien, D., *Learn to Remember: Transform your Memory Skills*, Duncan Baird Publishers, 2000.

O'Connor, J. & Seymour, J., *Introducing NLP*, 2nd edition, Aquarian/Thorsons, 1990.

Webster, R., *Winning Ways: In Search of your Best Performance*, Collins/Fontana, 1984.

Posture and movement

Aaberg, E., *Strength, Speed and Power*, Alpha, 2002.

Chek, P., *The Golf Biomechanics Manual: Whole in One Golf Conditioning*, C.H.E.K. Institute, 1999.

Francis, C., *Training for Speed*, Union Offset, 1997.

Kurtz, T., *Stretching Scientifically: A Guide to Flexibility Training*, 3rd edition, Stadion, 1994.

Parore, L., *Power Posture: The Foundation of Strength*, Apple Publishing, 2002.

Poliquin, C., *Modern Trends in Strength Training*, Poliquin, 2001.

Siff, M. C. & Verkhoshansky, Y. V, *Supertraining*, 4th edition, Supertraining International, 1999.

Tsatsouline, P., *Power to the People: Russian Strength Training Secrets for Everyday America*, Dragon Door Press, 1999.

Nutrition, fluid and sleep

Colgin, M., *All New Sports Nutrition Guide*, Apple Publishing, 2002.

Dement, W. C, *The Promise of Sleep*, Macmillan, 1999.

Noakes, T. D. & Durant, J. J., 'Physiological Requirements of Cricket', *Journal of Sports Sciences*, 18, 2000, pp. 919–29.

Siff, M. C & Yessis, M., *Sports Restoration and Massage: Secrets of the World's Greatest Superstars*, University of Witwatersrand, 1992.

Cricket

Bartlett, R. M., 'The Science and Medicine of Cricket: An Overview and Update', *Journal of Sport Sciences*, 21, 2003, pp. 733–52.

Batting

Barras, N., *Looking While Batting in Cricket: What A Coach Can Tell A Batsman*, Sports Coach, 1990, pp. 3–7.

Bates, W. H., *Better Eyesight Without Glasses*, Thorsons, 2000.

Bradman, D. G., *The Art of Cricket*, ETT Imprint, 1998, pp. 21–76, 142–7, 168–73.

Leonard, C. T., *The Neuroscience of Human Movement*, Mostly,1998.

Magill, R. A, *Motor Learning*, 5th edition, McGraw-Hill, 1998.

Renshaw, I. & Fairweather, M. M., 'Cricket Bowling Deliveries and the Discrimination Ability of Professional and Amateur Batters', *Journal of Sports Sciences*, 18, 2000, pp. 951–7.

Schmidt, R. A & Winsberg, G. A., *Motor Learning and Performance: From Principles to Practice*, 2nd edition, Human Kinetics, 2000.

Stretch, R. A., Bartlett, R. & Davids, K., 'A Review of Batting in Men's Cricket', *Journal of Sports Sciences*, 18, 2000, pp. 931–49.

Stretch, R., Buys, F., Du Toit, E. & Viljoen, G., Kinematics and Kinetics of the Drive Off the Front Foot in Cricket Batting, *Journal of Sports Sciences*, 16, 1998, pp. 711–20.

Shillinglaw, A. L, *Bradman Revisited – The Legacy of Sir Donald Bradman*, The Parrs Wood Press, 2003.

Watts, R. G. & Bahill, T. A., *Keep the Eye on the Ball*, W. H. Freeman & Company, 1990.

Whiting, H. T. A., *Input Characteristics, Acquiring Ball Skills: A Psychological Interpretation*, Bell & Sons, 1969, pp. 12–35.

Bowling

Bartlett, R. M., Stockill, N. P., Elliot, B. C. & Burnett, A. F., 'The Biomechanics of Fast Bowling in Men's Cricket: A Review', *Journal of Sports Sciences*, 14, 1995, pp. 403–24.

Bartlett, R. & Wood, D., *The Theory and Practice of Bowling 'Reverse Swing'*, Sports Coach, 1995.

Bradman, D. G., *The Art of Cricket*, ETT Imprint, 1998, pp. 77–140.

Elliot, B. C., 'Back Injuries and the Fast Bowler in Cricket', Journal of Sport Sciences, 18, 2000, pp. 983–91.

Elliot, B., Sakurai, S., Lloyd, D. & Besier, T., 'The Measurement of Shoulder Alignment in Cricket Fast Bowling', *Journal of Sports Sciences*, 20, pp. 507–10.

Glazier, P. S, Paradisis, G. P. & Cooper, S. M., 'Anthropometric and Kinematic Influences on Release Speed in Mens Fast-Medium Bowling', *Journal of Sports Sciences*, 18, 2000, pp. 1013–21.

Hurrion, P. D, Dyson, R. & Hale, T., 'Simultaneous Measurements of Back and Front Foot Ground Reaction Forces During the Same Delivery Stride of the Fast-Medium Bowler', *Journal of Sports Sciences*, 18, 2000, pp. 993–97.

Lillee, D. K. & Brayshaw, I., *The Art of Fast Bowling*, Williams Collins, 1977.

Lloyd, D. G, Anderson, J. & Elliot, B. C., 'An Upper Limb Kinematic Model for the Examination of Cricket Bowling: A Case Study of Mutah Muralitharan', *Journal of Sports Sciences*, 18, 2000, pp. 975–82.

Portius, M. R., Sinclair, P. J., Burke, S. T, Moore, D. J. A. & Farhart, P. J., 'Cricket Fast Bowling Performance and Technique and the Influence of Selected Physical Factors During an 8-Over Spell', *Journal of Sports Sciences*, 18, 2000, pp. 999–1011.

Wallis, R., Elliot, B. & Koh, M., The Effect of Fast Bowling Harness in Cricket: An Intervention Study, *Journal of Sports Sciences*, 20, 2002, pp. 495–506.

Wilkins, B., *Cricket: The Bowlers Art*, Kangaroo Press, 1997.

Fielding

Bradman, D. G., *The Art of Cricket*, ETT Imprint, 1998, pp. 148–59.

Cook, D. P. & Strike, S. C., 'Throwing in Cricket', *Journal of Sports Sciences*, 18, 2000, pp. 965–73.

Regan, D., 'Visual Factors in Hitting and Catching', *Journal of Sports Sciences*, 15(6), 1997, pp. 533–58.

Wicket-keeping

Bradman, D. G., *The Art of Cricket*, ETT Imprint, 1998, pp. 160–7.

Houlston, D. R. & Lowes, R. 'Anticipatory Cue-Utilisation Processes Amongst Expert and Non Expert Wicketkeepers in Cricket', *International Journal of Sports Psychology*, 24(1), 1993, pp. 59–73.

Captaincy

Bradman, D. G., *The Art of Cricket*, ETT Imprint, 1998, pp. 174–81.

Selection and talent identification

Bradman, D. G., *The Art of Cricket*, ETT Imprint, 1998, pp. 202–8.

Tichy, N. M. & Sherman, S., *Control your Destiny or Someone Else Will*, First HarperBusiness, 1993.